THE MOST ROMANTIC HOTELS and INNS in BRITAIN

THE MOST ROMANTIC HOTELS and INNS in BRITAIN

EDITED BY
RICHARD NISSEN

St. Martin's Press
New York

THE MOST ROMANTIC HOTELS AND INNS IN BRITAIN. Copyright © 1984 by Bedtime Books. All rights reserved. Printed in the United States of America. No part of this book may be used or reproduced in any manner whatsoever without written permission except in the case of brief quotations embodied in critical articles or reviews. For information, address St. Martin's Press, 175 Fifth Avenue, New York, N.Y. 10010.

Library of Congress Cataloging in Publication Data
Main entry under title:

The Most romantic hotels and inns in Britain.

   1. Hotels, taverns, etc.—Great Britain—Directories.
I. Nissen, Richard.
TX910.G7M67   1986   647'.94101   85-25165
ISBN 0-312-54919-9 (pbk.)

First published in Great Britain by Futura Publications.
First U.S. Edition
10 9 8 7 6 5 4 3 2 1

Acknowledgment

With especial thanks to the British Tourist Authority for all its help.

CONTRIBUTING REVIEWERS

Jeremy and Anne Amos

Stephen Brook

Sarah Fitzalan Howard

Sylviane Lacoste

Chris Lohan

Juliet Nissen

Anthony and Karen Nissen

Julia Vickerman

Additional illustrations by Alison Hoblyn

Contents

INTRODUCTION 11

HOW TO USE THIS BOOK 13

SCOTLAND 17

Ardanaiseig, Kilchrenan 18
The Clifton Hotel, Nairn 20
Cromlix House, Dunblane 22
Greywalls, Gullane 24
Inverlochy Castle, Fort William 26
Isle of Eriska, Ledaig 28
Johnstounburn Hotel, Humbie 30
Sunlaws, Kelso 32

THE NORTH 35

Hall Garth Country House, Coatham Mundeville,
    Co. Durham 36
Kirkby Fleetham Hall, Northallerton, N. Yorkshire 38
Michael's Nook, Grasmere, Cumbria 40
Miller Howe, Windermere, Cumbria 42
Sharrow Bay, Ullswater, Cumbria 44
White Moss House, Grasmere, Cumbria 46

WALES 49

Bodysgallen Hall Hotel, Llandudno, Gwynedd 50
The Crown Inn, Whitebrook, Gwent 52
Lake Vyrnwy, Llanwddyn, Salop 54
Llwynderw, Abergwesyn, Powys 56

CENTRAL ENGLAND 59

The Cottage in the Wood, Malvern, Worcestershire 60
Hambleton Hall, nr. Oakham, Leicestershire 62
Hope End Country House, Ledbury, Hereford 64
Mallory Court, Bishops Tachbrook, Warwickshire 66
Riber Hall, Matlock, Derby 68
Riverside Country House Hotel, Ashford-in-the-Water,
    Derby 70

THE COTSWOLDS 73

Buckland Manor, Broadway, Worcestershire 74
The Close, Tetbury, Glouestershire 76
Dormy House, Broadway, Worcestershire 78
The Gentle Gardener, Tetbury, Gloucestershire 80
The Greenway, Shurdington, Gloucestershire 82
Lords of the Manor Hotel, Upper Slaughter,
   Gloucestershire 84
Lower Brook House, Blockley, Worcestershire 86
The Lygon Arms, Broadway, Worcestershire 88
The Swan, Bibury, Gloucestershire 90

AVON 93

Homewood Park, Hinton Charterhouse, Avon 94
Hunstrete House, Chelwood, Avon 96
The Royal Crescent, Bath, Avon 98
Ston Easton Park, Farrington Gurney, Avon 100
Thornbury Castle, Thornbury, Avon 102

LONDON & HOME COUNTIES 105

The Bell Inn, Aston Clinton, Buckinghamshire 106
Blakes, London, SW7 108
11, Cadogan Gardens, London, SW3 110
The French Horn, Sonning, Berkshire 112
Lythe Hill Hotel, nr. Haslemere, Surrey 114
Number Sixteen Hotel, London, SW7 116
The Orient Express, London–Venice 118
The Ritz, London, W1 120
The Stafford, London, SW1 122

EAST ANGLIA 125

Congham Hall, Grimston, Norfolk 126
Maison Talbooth, Dedham, Essex 128
Priors Hall, Stebbing, Essex 130
Seckford Hall Hotel, Woodbridge, Suffolk 132
Shipdham Place, Shipdham, Norfolk 134
Swynford Paddocks, Newmarket, Suffolk 136

DEVON & CORNWALL 139

The Abbey Hotel, Penzance, Cornwall 140
Bly House, Chagford, Devon 142
Combe House, Gittisham, Devon 144
Gidleigh Park, Chagford, Devon 146
Half Moon Inn, Sheepwash, Devon 148
Riverside, Helford, Cornwall 150
Woodhayes, Whimple, Devon 152

THE SOUTH-WEST 155

Beechfield House, Beanacre, Wiltshire 156
Bishopstrow House, Warminster, Wiltshire 158
The Castle, Taunton, Somerset 160
Chedington Court, Beaminster, Dorset 162
Chewton Glen, New Milton, Hampshire 164
The Manor House, Castle Combe, Wiltshire 166
The Sign of the Angel, Lacock, Wiltshire 168
Tarr Steps Hotel, Hawkridge, Somerset 170

SUSSEX & KENT 173

Bailiffscourt Hotel, Climping, W. Sussex 174
Eastwell Manor, Ashford, Kent 176
Gravetye Manor, East Grinstead, E. Sussex 178
Little Thakeham, Storrington, W. Sussex 180
The Priory, Rushlake Green, E. Sussex 182
Stone Green Hall, Mersham, Kent 184

Index by Hotel 187

Index by Town 189

Authors' Biographies 191

Introduction

We scoured the country to come up with this relatively small list of hotels which we think have that special romantic ingredient. The hotels range from the grandest in the land to places which are really people's homes with just a few rooms. Within a few moments of walking through the front door we knew whether or not the hotel was for us. Our criterion for "romantic" was above all a sense of style and atmosphere. We had to be made to feel special and the setting had to touch our hearts.

We looked for a welcome when we arrived which made us feel comfortable and at home. We spoke to the owners or managers of each hotel and tried to gauge their characters and essentially their attitude to caring for the well-being of their guests. We made notes on the bedrooms. The first impression was terribly important. The room had to be pretty, clean and charming. Then we looked for crisp sheets, sweet-smelling soaps and thick towels in the bathrooms. We always liked to see a fresh posy of flowers in the room. Four-posters became a fetish and comfy mattresses a must.

Little touches make all the difference so we loved finding a pin cushion with needles and thread, a pomander in the wardrobe, or perhaps potpourri on the mantelpiece. A nice touch was a selection of books and a trouser press. We thoroughly applaud bottled water by the bedside, and a remote control on the TV. On the other hand we have not insisted on the TV or telephone—some of the most romantic hotels have neither. We felt that charm more than compensated in those few hotels that did not have a private bath in each room.

As for the hotel itself, the place had to have a charm of its own with views of the gardens if possible—all of which would make it a real pleasure to visit. Many of our hotels are run by their owners who have made each place reflect their own personalities. Often they have had no previous experience of the hotel trade and have based their establishments on the things they think important or that they would like to find if going away to stay themselves.

We truly believe that "food is the music of love," so we have often described in detail the meals we have eaten.

A romantic vacation isn't complete without a wonderful meal before you retire. Indeed, some of the most interesting cooking in England is being practised at the hotels we have included. There are those who are trying to create a typically English cuisine, others experimenting with nouvelle cuisine. All produce food which is out of the ordinary.

We have tried to bring out the special character of each hotel in our descrption, but all should make you feel special and give you a lovely holiday. Some of the hotels already have great reputations so you should book to avoid disappointment. Others we hope you will discover, as we have done, and reward their efforts and enthusiasm with a visit. We would like to hear of any place that you feel should be included in any future edition.

This is the book for discerning lovers who should browse through the book to pick the ideal spot for that special trip. We hope you enjoy yourselves.

Richard Nissen
Bedtime Books
Suites 101-110
35 Piccadilly
London W1V 9PB

How to Use This Book

1 The drawing gives you some idea of what sort of place to expect. Is it grand? Is it a castle? A picture tells a thousand words.

2 *Meals*

We have given the times of the meals to give you a guideline lest you should be passing and feeling famished. However, many hotels will do a simple dinner if you will be arriving late. As for breakfast, all the hotels provide a Continental breakfast in the rooms but in many you must go to the dining room for a full English breakfast. On the whole we think it is difficult to do a good cooked breakfast in the rooms as it is virtually impossible to keep the eggs and bacon hot if you are to enjoy your orange juice and cereal first. We also think that one of the charms of the hotels we have chosen is the fresh airy smell of the rooms—too many eggs, bacon and kippers in the rooms and the hotel gets that faintly greasy smell which merits instant disqualification from the book.

3 *Children and Dogs*

For our romantic vacations, we have been delighted to be told that both children and dogs are not welcome. However, we should add that frequently hotel keepers are happy to make exceptions for the well-behaved children and dogs which they know.

4 *Directions*

We have tried to give you a brief description of how to find the hotels. Many are difficult to find and you should always ask for more detailed directions when you book. Most hotels have maps which they will send to you with their brochures. The directions start from the nearest town.

5 *Special Features*

These are just a few words to get the feel of the place.

6 Price

Here we have tried to give you some idea of how much one night will cost. The price category is based on prices in force in summer 1985, and include the price of an average double room and typical dinner for two with a bottle of the house wine including service (where charged) and tax.

Beware: The best (often the most romantic) rooms and suites are frequently the most expensive and cost much more than the average. Equally, a few drinks at the bar, a bottle of champagne and a couple of brandies can bump up the bill enormously.

Prices: £ = to £75.00
££ = £75.00 to £110.00
£££ = £110.00 to £150.00
££££ = £150.00 and over

7 The "heart" check-list

This should give you an idea about the hotel at a glance. A closed heart ♥ represents exceptional quality, an open heart ♡ is for what is good and worth bringing to your attention.

Under the Amenities section a closed heart describes what is actually available on or from the hotel's premises; an open heart tells you what is available nearby.

Scotland

1. Ardanaiseig, Kilchrenan
2. The Clifton Hotel, Nairn
3. Cromlix House, Dunblane
4. Greywalls, Gullane
5. Inverlochy Castle, Fort William
6. Isle of Eriska, Ledaig
7. Johnstounburn House, Humbie
8. Sunlaws, Kelso

Ardanaiseig

Ardanaiseig
Kilchrenan
by Taynuilt
Argyll
Scotland
Tel: 08663 333

Managers: Michael and Frieda Yeo

Cards: All (deposit of £35.00)

15 rooms (8 twin, 7 double)

Dinner 7.30–9.00
Lunch 12.30–2.00
Breakfast 8.30–9.45

Children: Not under 8
Dogs: At discretion of management

Open: Easter to end October

Directions: From Oban take A85 to Taynuilt, turn right on to B845 for 5 miles to Kilchenan, follow signs to Ardanaiseig.

Special Features: Gardens; Friendly atmosphere; Beautiful views

Price: ££/£££ (bargain breaks available)

HOTEL: Buildings♡ Rooms♡ Food♡ Wine♡ Garden♥ Views♥
AMENITIES: Tennis♥ Swimming♥ Fishing♥ Riding♡ Croquet♥ Walks♥

18

It's not easy to get to Ardanaiseig – there's a four-mile drive down the single-track estate road – but it's well worth the effort. Michael and Frieda Yeo have recently created one of the most attractive country house hotels in Scotland. The 1834 house is gloriously situated on a promontory overlooking Loch Awe. The massive peaks of Argyll form a backdrop one could never weary of.

The rooms are delightfully light and cheerful. The Yeos are anxious above all else to please, and it shows. There's TV and radio in the rooms, fruit, bath oil, shower caps, the hotel's own soap, large towels, and complimentary sherry on arrival. Michael Yeo hopes the latter won't prevent you from coming down to the bar for a drink before dinner in the elegant candle-lit dining room. There's a set meal, but you can choose from an alternative list of house specialities if you prefer. We were delighted with the generous portions of good fresh food; the chef uses local produce whenever possible. The wine list is well balanced, with plenty of cheaper bottles. We took coffee in the lofty and beautiful drawing room with its grand piano and floor-to-ceiling windows looking on to the Loch. Mr Yeo will gladly introduce you to other guests if you wish or, equally, he'll leave you alone to enjoy your privacy.

Breakfast is a treat. Just order anything you want – trout, cutlets, even steak – and you'll probably get it. Breads and jams are all homemade.

Ardanaiseig is famous for its gardens, which are at their best in May and June. Attractive walks have been laid out both in the 50-acre Victorian garden and in the adjoining 2000-acre estate. There's even a 'secret garden' that Michael Yeo only shows to honeymooners, whom he likes to encourage. If during the day you want to play tennis but don't have your gear with you, or want to take a walk through the woods but left your wellies at home – don't worry: the Yeos will gladly lend you whatever you need. In poor weather you can also enjoy a game of snooker.

Gorgeous surroundings, good food, charming rooms, friendly service, discretion – what more could anyone want from a romantic hideaway? We can't imagine anyone leaving Ardanaiseig feeling discontented.

The Clifton Hotel

The Clifton Hotel
Nairn
Scotland
Tel: 0667 53119

Owner: J. Gordon Macintyre

Cards: All (no deposit)

13 rooms (7 double, 6 twin)

Dinner: From 7.00
Lunch: 12.30–2.30
Breakfast: Any time

Open: February to November

Directions: Off the A96, go down Marine road towards Inverness, Clifton is on the corner of Seafield Street on the lefthand side.

Special Features: Victorian decor; Great style

Price: ££

HOTEL: Rooms♥ Food♥ Wine♥ Views♡
AMENITIES: Tennis♡ Swimming♡ Fishing♡ Golf♡ Riding♡ Beach♡ Sailing♡ Walks♡

20

Walk into the Clifton and you could be forgiven for thinking you've stumbled on to the set for a Victorian melodrama. Its exotic furnishings and flamboyant colour schemes mark out the Clifton as a very special hotel, but the genial eccentricity of the owner, Gordon Macintyre, does not prevent him and his staff from providing the warmest of welcomes and the best of service.

The bedrooms are startling and beautiful, decorated in high style. No two are alike. Immense beds jostle with antique furnishings, Oriental chests, embroidered cushions, thick carpets and heavy curtains, fresh flower arrangements and swirling fabric designs. It's less crazy than it sounds, as Mr Macintyre has an excellent eye and firm, if unusual, taste. There are no phones or TV sets in the rooms, but a portable radio is provided on request. Room No. 7 boasts a gargantuan four-poster. One oddity: baths are not partitioned off, but, after a night of passion, it may be handy to step from bed to bath unimpeded.

The drawing room is full of family portraits – indeed, every wall of the house is filled with pictures – tall potted plants, bibelots, and a bright hand-blocked wallpaper identical to that used in the Palace of Westminster in 1849. The dining room (which doubles as a recital hall in winter months) is surrounded by plate-glass windows overlooking the Firth. With all the candles lit and the glassware gleaming on the lace tablecloths, the effect is magically theatrical.

The cooking, classical French in style, is among the finest in northern Scotland. There's a lunchtime menu of seafood only, including oysters that the Clifton keeps in special tanks. Lunch is served in a lovely green room, with antique silver laid over white linen tablecloths. The chef will gladly supply special dishes on request, especially vegetarian ones. Alternatively you can lunch in the bar over an omelette or a venison or salmon salad. The wine list is superb: 160 bins, constantly changing.

Breakfast in your room as late as you like. Gordon Macintyre positively encourages romance and seclusion, which may be why guests return regularly to this unique and colourful hotel.

Cromlix House

Cromlix House
Dunblane
Perthshire FK15 9JT
Scotland
Tel: 0786 822125

Manager: Stephen Coupe

Cards: All

10 rooms (4 doubles, 6 suites)

Dinner: From 7.30
Lunch: By arrangement
Breakfast: 8.00–9.30

Open: Year-round

Disabled guests welcome

Directions: Cromlix lies 4 miles north of Dunblane, just north of the village of Kinbuck

Special Features: 5000-acre estate; Large luxurious rooms

Price: ££

HOTEL: Buildings♥ Rooms♥ Food♡ Wine♥ Garden♡ View♡
AMENITIES: Tennis♥ Fishing♥ Golf♡ Riding♥ Croquet♥ Walks♥

The first impression of Cromlix House is a sombre one: a dark, hefty Victorian pile in the midst of a 5000-acre estate. Fortunately, the interior is far more cheerful, and the bedrooms are among the most luxurious to be found anywhere. Indeed, so grand is the layout that suites outnumber ordinary double bedrooms. Cromlix was a private house until a few years ago, and the family, who still live on the estate, left behind much splendid old furniture and porcelain.

Even in summer you're likely to find log fires blazing in either of the two main drawing rooms. In fine weather you can sit in the conservatory, and in foul weather retreat to the well-stocked library upstairs. With only 20 guests to share this mansion, there's no lack of privacy. On request Mr Coupe will arrange a candle-lit dinner *à deux* in front of a roaring fire – that's dining in the grandest, most romantic style.

The bedrooms are superb, especially the two turret suites with their large rooms off a private corridor and beautiful views over the pleasant gardens on to the surrounding hills. The rooms aren't exactly beautiful; they are too imposing for that. But they are spacious, light, enormously comfortable, and furnished appropriately for a house of this kind. We really did feel like pampered guests in a stately home. All rooms have TV, Roger & Gallet soaps, bath oils, huge towels, Malvern water and a writing desk.

There's no bar, but drinks are served in a lemon-walled drawing room, together with lobster vol-au-vents and hot toasted almonds. A five-course set dinner is served in the formal dining room on tables heavy with family silver and Wedgwood bone china. The wine list is as sumptuous as the hotel. After coffee we mounted the grand staircase to our suite where we found the bed turned down, curtains drawn, lamps switched on and an electric blanket warming the bed. In the morning we enjoyed a traditional Scottish breakfast of salmon kedgeree.

Cromlix is for those who want complete seclusion in the lap of luxury. Here, you can hide from the world in the timeless atmosphere of a well-run country mansion.

Greywalls

Greywalls
Gullane
E. Lothian EH31 2EG
Scotland
Tel: 0620 842144
Telex: PREHTL 727396

Manager: John Robson

Cards: All (deposit £20.00 per person)

23 rooms (1 double, 17 twins)

Dinner: 7.30–9.00
Lunch: 12.30–2.00
Breakfast: 8.00–9.30

Children and dogs: At discretion of management

Open: Year-round

Directions: Find hotel signs on the A198 at the east end of Gullane

Special Features: Golf course; Lutyens's house; Super food

Price: £££ (bargain breaks available)

HOTEL: Buildings♡ Food♥ Wine♥ Garden♡
AMENITIES: Tennis♥ Swimming♡ Fishing♡ Golf♥ Riding♡ Beach♡ Sailing♡ Croquet♥ Walks♡

This delightful butterfly-shaped house was designed by the great Edwardian architect, Lutyens, and, a further bonus, the gardens were laid out by his frequent associate, Gertrude Jekyll. So it's not surprising that Greywalls is an utterly charming hotel of great character. Built with an eye to domesticity and comfort, it offers luxury on an intimate scale.

The ground floor provides a string of public rooms, all comfortable without being overly formal. There's a delightful garden room and a large library with hundreds of books for guests to browse through. We had no trouble finding quiet corners in this hotel. From many of these rooms you can step straight out into the lovely walled gardens which fan out behind the house.

Upstairs are the bedrooms, and more rooms are provided in the tactful new extension. They are all light, airy and cheerful, with views either on to the garden or the golf course and the sea just a few hundred yards beyond. Note that most of the rooms have twin beds. Every room is provided with fruit, fresh flowers, Scottish spring water, a hairdryer, and a radio, but no TV.

The bar was crowded so we drank aperitifs in the library and nibbled hot hors d'oeuvres. The stylish dining rooms overlook the golf course. Using top-quality ingredients, mostly produced locally, Greywalls specializes in nouvelle cuisine. We revelled in an exquisite hot sole terrine and tender pink duck. Greywalls offers a reasonably priced set meal of five courses, though you can eat à la carte if you prefer. The wine list is magnificent – over 200 bins – with some bargains at the top of the range, but the house wines are perfectly adequate. After coffee and petit-fours we retreated to our comfortable bedroom and slept soundly until our cooked breakfast arrived.

For many, Greywalls's chief attraction will be that it adjoins the famous Muirfield golf course. Don't be surprised if you find Jack Nicklaus in the dining room! For non-golfers too there's plenty to do: fishing, tennis, walking, sightseeing, visiting the nearby castles, or just staying indoors to enjoy the comforts and amenities of this easy-going and distinctive hotel.

Inverlochy Castle

Inverlochy Castle
Fort William
Scotland
Tel: 0397 2177/8

Manager: Michael Leonard

Cards: All (deposit of one night's stay required)

14 rooms (2 suites, 12 doubles)

Dinner: 8.00
Lunch: 12.30–2.00
Breakfast: 7.30–9.30, but 24-hour service

Dogs: No

Open: April 1 to early November (book well in advance)

Directions: Inverlochy Castle is situated 3 miles north of Fort William, just off the road to Inverness

Special Features: Setting and grounds; Excellent food and wine; Luxurious rooms

Price: ££££

HOTEL: Buildings♥ Rooms♥ Food♥ Wine♥ Garden♥ Views♥
AMENITIES: Tennis♥ Fishing♥ Riding♡ Sailing♡ Walks♥

Arriving at this Scottish baronial estate took our breath away on two counts: the sea of rhododendrons that line the driveways and the immense two-storey hall of the castle. It's so vast that even the grand piano in the corner is easy to overlook. Antique cradles are filled with flowers, and logs crackle in the great fireplace. A painted ceiling floats overhead. The hall sets the tone for this sumptuous hotel. For all its size, Inverlochy is immaculate. A staff of over 50 looks after 28 guests, and we watched in awe as maids nonchalantly removed specks from carpets and fallen petals from tables.

The bedrooms are equally luxurious. Extra-wide double beds (they can be converted into twin beds if you prefer) only take up a small part of these large, well-kept rooms, and some of the bathrooms are almost as spacious. There are showers as well as baths, and all the choice items you'd expect: Malvern water, Rochas soaps and bath oils, and, of course, TV. For truly lazy lovers, there's no need to get up at all, as there's comprehensive room service at all times. Many rooms have two sets of doors to ensure maximum privacy and quiet.

The five-course dinners are served in the beautiful dining room that overlooks the hotel's private loch. The chef trained at the Connaught, so the cooking – using only the finest ingredients, including vegetables grown at the castle – is of the highest standard. So is the magnificent wine list, with its superb range of clarets and burgundies. After dinner take coffee in the hall or the lovely drawing room lined with rococo mirrors and old paintings. Or go upstairs for a game of billiards – but mind the antlers on the walls!

After breakfast explore the 50-acre garden or shop in nearby Fort William or climb Ben Nevis. Or stay in bed till lunch, which is served by white-coated waiters in a second dining room, less imposing than the main one but equally attractive. In fine weather, have lunch or tea on the terrace.

At Inverlochy you can confidently expect the best, since this beautiful and fastidious luxury hotel is keen to maintain its high reputation. Michael Leonard, or the regal owner, Mrs Greta Hobbs, are always around to cater to all of your whims.

Isle of Eriska

Isle of Eriska
Ledaig
Connel
Argyll PA37 15D
Scotland
Tel: 063172 371
Telex: 727396 Attn. Erıska

Owners: Robin and Sheena Buchanan-Smith

Cards: Americn Express (deposit required)

15 double rooms (11 twin, 4 double)

Dinner: 7.30–8.30
Lunch: 1.00–1.30
Breakfast: 8.30–9.30

Dogs: At discretion of management

Open: End March to end October

Directions: From Oban take the A828 towards Fort William. Then look for Isle of Eriska signs on left after Ledaig.

Special Features: Carnival atmosphere; Own island

Disabled guests welcome

Price: £££ (Bargain breaks available)

HOTEL: Buildings♡ Rooms♡ Food♡ Wine♡ Garden♡ Views♡
AMENITIES: Tennis♥ Swimming♥ Fishing♥ Riding♥ Sailing♡ Croquet♥ Walks♥

Cross the little bridge from the mainland and you suddenly find yourself in a world apart: the 300-acre Isle of Eriska. As Robin Buchanan-Smith who owns this Scottish baronial estate puts it, 'The Isle of Eriska belongs to my guests.' The personality of this former university chaplain dominates this splendid hotel. In the evening his burly form elegantly swirls round the public rooms, greeting all his guests; and in the mornings, sporting his kilt, he's there to advise guests on outings and the weather. Most of Eriska's guests are regulars, who return for up to three weeks at a time.

We could see why. The atmosphere is so relaxed that enjoyment is contagious. The staff greet you by name and are genuinely eager to help and please. This attentive service isn't obtrusive. It's easy to escape for a game of tennis or for some fishing or a stroll along the shore.

The rooms vary from simply furnished, medium-sized doubles to a handful of enormous rooms. We'd recommend spending a little more, especially for a long stay, to enjoy one of the larger rooms, such as Jura, Skye, Coll, Shuna or Soay. All rooms are equipped with kettles, mending kits, aspirin, a trouser press, fruit and good soaps. TV is available on request.

Eriska is run like a house rather than a hotel. A gong announces the six-course set dinner; simple alternatives can be provided. The main course is usually a roast brought to your table on a splendid carving trolley. The owner's wife Sheena supervises the cooking, which is based on fresh ingredients, such as local prawns. Breads are homemade. After dinner we took a romantic walk in the gardens; remember that in summer in Scotland it's still light at 11.

Continental breakfast can be served in your room, but make just one trip down in the morning to help yourself to the hearty Scottish breakfast. Later, buffet lunches are served, and morning coffee and afternoon tea are on the house.

Eriska may not be to everyone's taste. It's comfortable, friendly, gregarious, even rambunctious. We delighted in this comfortable hotel that has no pretensions but dedicates itself to making its guests welcome and contented. If you want haute cuisine and dignified seclusion, go elsewhere. But if you want a memorable, convivial weekend in addition to romance, then go to Eriska.

Johnstounburn House

Johnstounburn House
Humbie
E. Lothian EH36 5PL
Scotland
Tel: 087533 696
Telex: 727897

Special Features: Pretty countryside; Historic house

Open: Year-round

Price: ££

Manager: Matthew L. Wylie

Cards: All (£20.00 deposit per person)

11 rooms (2 double, 9 twin)

Dinner: 8.00
Lunch: 12.00–2.00 (bar lunch)
Breakfast: 8.00–9.30

Dogs: At discretion of management

Directions: Head for Humbie and find the signs.

HOTEL: Buildings♥ Rooms♡ Food♡ Garden♥ Views♥
AMENITIES: Fishing♡ Golf♡ Riding♡ Croquet♥ Walks♡

Only 15 miles from Edinburgh, Johnstounburn House is set in a fold of the gentle Lammermuir Hills. Built in 1625, the grand but not forbidding mansion was rescued from dilapidation by the Vere Nicolses in 1980 and they have now created a comfortable and appealing country hotel.

The rooms are not especially large – with the exception of the splendid Lammermuir Room with its views on to two sides of the gardens. Unusually, the attic rooms are among the most attractive, uncluttered and decorated with a light touch. If you want a double bed, be sure to specify; there are only two at Johnstounburn, and both are in rather small rooms.

The principal public rooms are on the first floor, reminding us that this was a private house until recently. The dining room dates from 1740 and is gloriously panelled. Pink table linen and candles, fresh flowers and delicate glassware help to give this lovely room a wonderfully romantic aura. Raymond Baudon has been the chef here since the beginning, and his dishes are sturdily French in style though not without his personal touches. All ingredients are fresh and of high quality, and he's happy to prepare special dishes at your request. The wine list is small but with a good selection of inexpensive but reliable bottles.

After dinner everyone takes coffee in the spacious Cedar Room, another panelled drawing room, so comfortably furnished that we were tempted to sit and stay, sampling more of the numerous malt whiskies available. Classical Muzak is piped into some of the public rooms; it's unobtrusive, but unnecessary in a hotel as comfortable and atmospheric as Johnstounburn.

In the morning we woke to the gentle sound of sheep on the hills. After Continental breakfast in bed, we eased into the day with a walk round the large and beautiful garden, surrounded by walls and high hedges, and visited the historic dovecote in the park. There's fine countryside and ancient castles to be visited in good weather, and in inclement weather it's a short drive into Edinburgh.

Johnstounburn is a calm and relaxed hotel, beautifully situated, secluded but not cut off. It offers good value and our stay was enhanced by the friendliness and professionalism of the youthful staff.

Sunlaws

Sunlaws House Hotel
Kelso
Roxburghshire TD5 8JZ
Scotland
Tel: Roxburgh (05735) 331

Manager: Allan Hobkirk

Cards: All

14 rooms (5 doubles, 5 twins)

Dinner: 7.30–9.30 (children's suppers: 5.30–6.00)
Lunch: 12.30–2.00 (bar lunch)
Breakfast: 8.00–9.30 (Sun: 9.00–10.00)
Meals can be arranged at all hours.

Children and Dogs: Welcomed

Open: Year-round

Directions: From Kelso take the B6352 towards Town Yetholm. Turn right on to the A698, go through Heiton, Sunlaws on right

Special Features: 200 acres of grounds; Conservatory; Sporting pursuits

Price: £

HOTEL: Buildings♡ Rooms♡ Garden♥
AMENITIES: Tennis♡ Fishing♥ Golf♡ Riding♡

For country house seclusion and a charming Scottish welcome, Sunlaws House is certainly a place to consider for a peaceful and romantic weekend. The house, built in about 1880, stands in 200 acres of delightful grounds – rolling lawns, duck ponds, mature trees and some fine Himalayan and other plants, all combine to give Sunlaws the feeling of a gracious country house. It forms part of the Duke of Roxburghe's estate and was opened in September 1982 under the management of Allan Hobkirk, with the close personal interest of the Duke and Duchess. This becomes increasingly apparent during one's stay, as one strolls around the house and grounds. The old library, which is now a bar, still retains the original bookshelves and is furnished with books from the Duke's collection at nearby Floors Castle. The wines mainly come from the ducal cellars, the attractive decorations of the bedrooms were chosen by the Duchess, fish and game from the estate are regularly on the menu – these are just a few examples of the owners' involvement. The resulting impression is one of good taste, country house comfort and the atmosphere of an earlier age, with little to remind one of the late 20th century except, perhaps, highly efficient heating!

We were given a large and very comfortable room with a balcony overlooking the garden – for one's peaceful moments – and remote control TV for one's noisier entertainment. Every room has its own bathroom, equipped with soft and enormous towels – a rare treat.

The menus are not particularly ambitious but very good, well-cooked dishes with seasonal game and fish a speciality and delicious home-grown vegetables. For those with a sporting as well as a romantic inclination, there is an opportunity for trout and sea-trout fishing on a three-mile stretch of the River Treviot – for no extra charge. For those who prefer spending their time more restfully, one can relax with a drink, a meal or just a good book in the charming conservatory.

All in all you will be enchanted by Sunlaws and its exceptional surroundings and you will find it hard to leave this beautiful and – were it not for its noble owners – peerless retreat.

The North

1 Hall Garth Country House, Coatham Mundeville, Co. Durham
2 Kirkby Fleetham Hall, Northallerton, N. Yorkshire
3 Michael's Nook, Grasmere, Cumbria
4 Miller Howe, Windermere, Cumbria
5 Sharrow Bay, Ullswater, Cumbria
6 White Moss House, Grasmere Cumbria

Hall Garth Country House

Hall Garth Country House Hotel
Coatham Mundeville
Darlington
Co Durham DL1 3LU
Tel: Aycliffe (0325) 313333

Resident proprietors: E. Williamson and J. Crocker

Cards: AMX, Access, Visa

19 rooms (14 doubles, of which 4 are four-poster, the best are Nos. 8 and 5, one is in the stables; 1 twin)

Dinner: 7.30–9.15
Lunch: 12.15–1.30
Breakfast: 7.30–9.30 (Sun 8.30–10.00)
English in dining room. Early morning tea from 7.30/Sun 8.30

Children: Welcomed

Dogs: Not allowed in public rooms or unattended in bedrooms

Open: 2 January to 24 December

Directions: Take Exit from A1(M) north of Darlington: A167. Take first turning left to Brafferton on road to Darlington

Special Features: Nice house; Warm welcome

Price: ££

HOTEL: Buildings♡ Rooms♡ Food♡ Wine♡ Garden♡
AMENITIES: Swimming♥ Golf♡ Riding♡ Croquet♡

Just outside Darlington doesn't at first sound a very promising place for a pretty country-house hotel. Hall Garth is one of those lived-in houses which was begun in 1540, the central part with the reception rooms and main bedrooms added in the 1650s and the last bit a sympathetic Victorian addition.

Some of the bedrooms open off the 17th-century stair with its heavy balustrade and open well. They still have their original deep panelled and solid doors, so there can be no question of the smallest squeak being overheard. We slept in bedroom eight, which is an airy sunny room overlooking the lawn, a little stream and the old deer park. You cannot see the folly which was the deer shelter from the window; you must explore for that. The little sitting room has a comfy sofa inviting you to cuddle up for a spot of TV before moving to the four-poster bed. We noted a lovely piece of local embroidery on cream watered silk at the bedhead and the pretty Durham quilted eiderdown before that slipped off the bed.

The nicest rooms are in the house but some of the bedrooms and one of the four-poster rooms are in the stables a little way from the house, which has also been converted into a country pub below. For the lazy this means you can take a pint and a ploughman's lunch with the locals under an umbrella in the garden near the stables; for the energetic, a frolic in the heated swimming pool followed by a sauna.

The hotel is owned and run by Ernest Williamson and Janice Crocker, both ex-teachers, whose baptism by fire to the catering business was to turn a pub in a pit village into a very successful restaurant. The cooking is good English fare: for our dinner we chose spiced jellied prawns and mushrooms followed by braised beef with celery, orange and walnuts and then chocolate rum cake. From their nice wine list we chose a bottle of Chateau Haut Bailly '73, which was good and inexpensive.

The hotel has ten acres of garden with its dovecote and makes an ideal base to visit the moors. You will like the welcome and enthusiasm of the owners and Mr Williamson's daughter, Heather, who soon makes you feel at home.

Kirkby Fleetham Hall

Kirkby Fleetham Hall
Kirkby Fleetham
Nr Northallerton
N. Yorks DL7 0SU
Tel: Northallerton (0609) 748226

Owners: David and Chris Grant

Cards: Visa, American Express, Diners (but cheques preferred)

19 rooms (13 doubles with private bath, including 2 four-posters)

Dinner: 7.00–9.00
Breakfast: 8.30–9.30 (or later by arrangement)
Lunch: 12.15–1.30 on Sun (other days by arrangement)

Children: Allowed

Dogs: By prior arrangement

Open: Year-round

Directions: Leave A1 at Leeming Bar (A684 exit). Follow signs for Great Fencote and Kirkby Fleetham, *not* Northallerton. The hotel is off a small road just beyond Kirkby Fleetham

Special Features: Set in James Herriot country; Nr Castle Howard (setting of 'Brideshead Revisited') and many other places of interest; 12th-century church next to the hotel; Several racecourses nearby

Price: ££

HOTEL: Buildings♥ Rooms♥ Food♥ Wine♥ Garden♥ Views♥
AMENITIES: Riding♡ Walks♥

Warmth is the keynote of Kirkby Fleetham Hall: this attractive house, remodelled in the late 18th century and lovingly restored by the Grants, is well heated to give protection from the chill Yorkshire winds; the colour scheme is warm and well attuned to the fine architectural features; moreover, the Grants will give you a warm welcome and take great pride in describing the delights which Yorkshire has to offer. This is James Herriot country: moorland punctuated by historic houses and other interesting places. For a weekend stay you might just walk through miles of woods and moors, perhaps bird-watching, visiting pubs and trying the local 'Old Peculier' ale. You will be tempted to stay longer, using the hotel as a base for exploring the area.

The finely proportioned building overlooks a lake and fields beyond. Indoors you will find comfort and informality. The Grants clearly love this house and find the challenge of running it as an efficient hotel yet maintaining its home-like atmosphere most rewarding. Their enthusiasm is infectious and it isn't surprising that guests frequently return.

On the menu are the words: 'Eating is like making love: it should be entered into with abandon – or not at all.' Chris Grant does all the cooking and she enjoys planning an imaginative menu, making the most of fresh ingredients and giving excellent value for money. The wine list is good and David knows a great deal about wines.

The rooms are very pretty and are all named after birds. Duvets protect one from cold Yorkshire nights, and a cheerful local lady brings a large breakfast in the morning. All rooms are large, well furnished and all possible needs are provided for. There are two four-posters.

All the decor has been chosen and, indeed, done by David and Chris Grant. The colours, fabrics and furniture suit the house so well that people often ask whether they had to do much to it, not realizing how it had been neglected before the Grants bought it. They work continuously to ensure the smooth running of the Hall in all respects, yet do so unobtrusively and cheerfully. What an achievement!

Michael's Nook

Michael's Nook
Grasmere
Nr Ambleside
Cumbria LA22 9RP
Tel: Grasmere (09665) 496

Resident Proprietors: Reg and Elizabeth Gifford

Cards: AMX

10 rooms (7 doubles, 3 twins)

Dinner: 7.30 for 8.00 (incl. in room rate)
Lunch: Must book. Packed also available
Breakfast: 8.45–9.30

Children: Not under 12

Dogs: By arrangement

Open: Year-round

Directions:
Approaching Grasmere from Ambleside on the A591, take the lane up to the right between the White Building – The Swan, and the car park

Special Features: Pretty garden; Croquet lawn; Lovely walks

Price: ££/£££

HOTEL: Buildings♡ Rooms♡ Food♥ Wine♥ Garden♥ Views♥
AMENITIES: Swimming♡ Fishing♡ Riding♡ Sailing♡ Croquet♥ Walks♥

The Lake District is so much the open hills and long hearty walks with wonderful views that it comes as a surprise to swing off the main road up a little lane to discover a Michael's Nook nestling in its own little haven of peace and beauty. Here is a garden of grassy slopes and clumps of decorative Japanese Maples surrounded by high trees and thickets of shrubs.

We were immediately offered, and accepted, a bottle of champagne on the terrace. The champagne went to our heads and the setting to our hearts; the smell of the flowers drifted up, the bees buzzed, a huge furry cat purred at our feet and a Great Dane occasionally licked a drooping finger.

We drifted into the intimate deep crimson dining room to delight in a quiet, wonderful dinner: a courgette soufflé with garlic mayonnaise (balanced and clever), then chicken liver and flageolet soup (unusual and delicate), a poached darne of fresh Scotch salmon, finished by a passion fruit soufflé with a raspberry coulis. The whole meal was delicate and refined with the sauces never too intrusive. Here, suddenly, was a meal where the underlying concepts of the new French cuisine had been completely mastered by Reg Gifford and his two chefs Paul Vidic and Phillip Vickery. After dinner we found a pair of comfortable armchairs in a bay window of the elegant drawing room where we sipped our coffee as the day slipped away with the changing colours of sunset.

Each of the ten bedrooms is different in its own way, but all are named after birds (each is painted on the door). Although it didn't have a double bed, we loved 'Woodpecker' with its original Victorian mahogany beds which also matched the wardrobe and bedside tables. This room has that old-fashioned charm of a guest bedroom in a country house. It is nicely proportioned and with a pleasant cornice. It gave us a feeling of restful serenity. With the windows open, the sounds of the night drifted up as we fell asleep.

Miller Howe

Miller Howe
Rayrigg Road
Windermere
Cumbria LA23 1EY
Tel: Windermere (09662) 2536

Chef and patron: John Tovey

Cards: AMX and Diners

13 rooms (9 twins, 4 doubles)

Dinner: 8.30. Open to non-residents
Lunch: Packed available
Breakfast: 9–9.30. English in dining room only

Children: Not under 12

Dogs: Not in public rooms

Directions: Take the A592 (Rayrigg Road) north out of Bowness (Windermere). Miller Howe is about 1 mile on left hand side

Special Features: Breathtaking view; Wonderful food; Great atmosphere

Price: ££/£££

HOTEL: Buildings♡ Rooms♡ Food♥ Wine♥ Views♥
AMENITIES: Tennis♡ Swimming♡ Fishing♡ Golf♡ Riding♡ Sailing♡ Walks♥

Miller Howe is orientated towards the spectacular Lake Windermere with little boats on the water and the view of the distant hills changing in colour and mood all through the day. We were lucky to witness the most superb sunset as we sat drinking an aperitif before dinner listening to classical music.

The place is inimitably John Tovey's, the ebullient patron and chef. He has created from this marvellous setting something which is totally his own and rightly renowned for its atmosphere and cuisine. The furniture is comfortable and eclectic with padded Chesterfields, statuettes of Napoleon's marshals, a case of Bristol glass and innumerable items which have caught John Tovey's fancy.

Before dinner everyone (some 70 people) gathers for a drink, savours the view and the virtuoso menu (there is no choice) and chooses their wine. Mr Tovey has a particular penchant for South African wines and has a special wine list explaining all, as well as his selection for that evening.

The lights dim and everyone is ushered into the dining room with its murals of Italy and its seating orientated towards the view framed by a couple of kissing cherubs over the fountain. Nothing could be more romantic.

The dinner is served with quick professionalism. A real team spirit reigns at the Miller Howe: the girl who greeted you as you arrived is serving your dinner, and you will probably meet her again cleaning your room in the morning.

John Tovey is famous for his cookbooks and some of his recipes appear in his dinners. We loved his individual style of cooking with seven interesting vegetable dishes, surrounding his roast pork stuffed with prunes, ginger and pistachio nuts with a calvados apple sauce and a tomato mustard cream sauce. We started with a summer savoury, then Lakeland mutton broth followed by trout with hazelnuts before we reached the pork. You finish with a choice of puddings – we had clafoutis Limousin.

The bedrooms have the view. There is a TV socket for those who must and travel Scrabble with a dictionary for rainy days. It is very comfortable, even Buck's Fizz before breakfast. Miller Howe remains for all who visit a memorable experience.

Sharrow Bay

The Sharrow Bay Country House Hotel
Ullswater
Nr Penrith
Cumbria
CA10 2LZ
Tel: Pooley Bridge (08536) 301/483

Proprietors: Francis Coulson and Brian Sack

Cards: None

30 rooms (9 doubles, 15 twins – 12 in house, 7 in Bankside)

Dinner: 8.00–8.30
Lunch: 1.00–1.30
Breakfast: 9.00–9.30

Children: None under 13

Dogs: No

Open: First Fri in March to First Mon in December

Directions: Leave the M6 at exit 40. Take the A66 to Keswick. Turn left on A592 to Pooley Bridge, go through it and turn right to Martingdale. The Sharrow Bay is a few miles on by the Lake.

Special Features: Superb views; Wonderful atmosphere and food

Price: £££

HOTEL: Buildings♥ Rooms♥ Food♥ Wine♥ Garden♥ Views♥
AMENITIES: Swimming♡ Fishing♡ Riding♡ Walks♥

The Sharrow Bay is the creation of two remarkable men: Francis Coulson and Brian Sack. It all started in 1948, while Francis Coulson was recuperating from an illness; he discovered the Sharrow Bay and knew this was to be his future. Gradually the hotel developed, rooms were added as money became available and the cooking gained a wider and wider reputation under Francis Coulson's direction. The Sharrow Bay is the reflection of these two men's vision, personalities and creativity. From their original concept the country house hotel movement was really born.

They are humble men, constantly concerned for the welfare of their guests. Their motto from the outset: to nurture, nourish and cosset people. Brian Sack is insistent that 'the Sharrow' is a home with the cushions crooked enough to feel comfortable. Francis Coulson's food stems from what he refers to as the gentle art of cooking carried out with a light heart and humility. The result is a memorable stay in an idyllic spot overlooking Ullswater. We saw a duck and her chicks paddle past the dining room window at breakfast.

The House itself has 12 bedrooms with 'Pinkie' and 'Silver' being the most romantic, beautifully decorated with their lovely views over the lake and the hills beyond. But then there is Bank House, a little self-contained place of its own further along Ullswater with another spectacular view. We had a wonderful tea on the terrace there. There are also rooms at the Lodge and in the Cottage. Some of the rooms do not have their own baths, but this seems irrelevant.

The food at the Sharrow Bay is superb with its five courses and 22 starters to choose from. We chose the perfect beef consommé, then we had fillet of fresh Aberdeen sole Adrienne, the Sharrow fresh fruit sorbet, and casserole of peppered Scottish rumpsteak and finished with the sticky toffee sponge with cream.

I could describe endlessly the crowded furniture, the embroidered sheets and extra thick towels, but it is the warm and wonderful experience of the Sharrow Bay that makes this place unique.

White Moss House

White Moss House
Rydal Water
Grasmere
Cumbria
LA22 9SE
Tel: Grasmere (09665) 295

Proprietors: Butterworth and Dixon Family

Cards: None

5 rooms (all doubles plus Brockstone Cottage)

Dinner: 7.30 for 8.00
Lunch: Packed available
Breakfast: 8.45–9.30 Early morning tea, English in dining room only

Directions: Between Grasmere and Ambleside on A591, overlooking Rydal Water.

Special Features: Brockstone Cottage; Great views

Price: ££

HOTEL: Rooms♡ Food♥ Wine♥ Views♥
AMENITIES: Swimming♡ Fishing♡ Golf♡ Riding♡ Sailing♡ Walks♡

White Moss House is a small hotel which started out as a simple bed and breakfast establishment but has turned into a place of pilgrimage for gourmets. It is a real family hotel owned and run by Arthur Butterworth and his wife Jean with their daughter Susan and her husband Peter Dixon, who gave up their jobs to help in the hotel. There can be few hotels with so many qualifications outside catering amongst the staff. The cooking is done by Jean Butterworth and Peter Dixon while Mr Butterworth and Susan Dixon look after the guests.

We arrived in the afternoon to be greeted by Susan Dixon's nanny who was running the reception and just happens to speak four languages fluently. She showed us to our charming room with a lovely view of Rydal Water. Each room has everything from walking routes to weighing scales and potpourri. Before dinner we visited their cottage, 'Brockstone', part of the hotel yet separate up in the woods behind the house. Here the view is magnificent and its isolated beauty makes it a truly romantic spot, where you can fend for yourself and yet enjoy the delicious dinner in the hotel.

The menu changes daily; that day we were spoiled with a courgette soup, avocado with curry cream sauce and poppadums, guinea fowl braised on a bed of apples with herbs and cider, Mrs Beeton's chocolate pudding and then the English cheeses. We drank a superb bottle of Clos des Jacobins, St Emilion '75 which had all the beauty of a good claret and with none of the acidity. When the cheeses came we were delighted, as many of them were firsts for us and were all matched by Mr Butterworth's choice of wine. We discovered they were real farmhouse cheeses culled from remote farms, one, Cotherstone, comes from Barnard Castle.

We really loved White Moss House: it was friendly, intimate, charming and delicious. Enjoy the lovely views and beautiful walks on the hill and circling Rydal Water; we could think of no more romantic place than 'Brockstone'. You are encouraged to spend more than three nights at White Moss, and you would be crazy not to. Here is something special: a family striving and achieving the very highest standards.

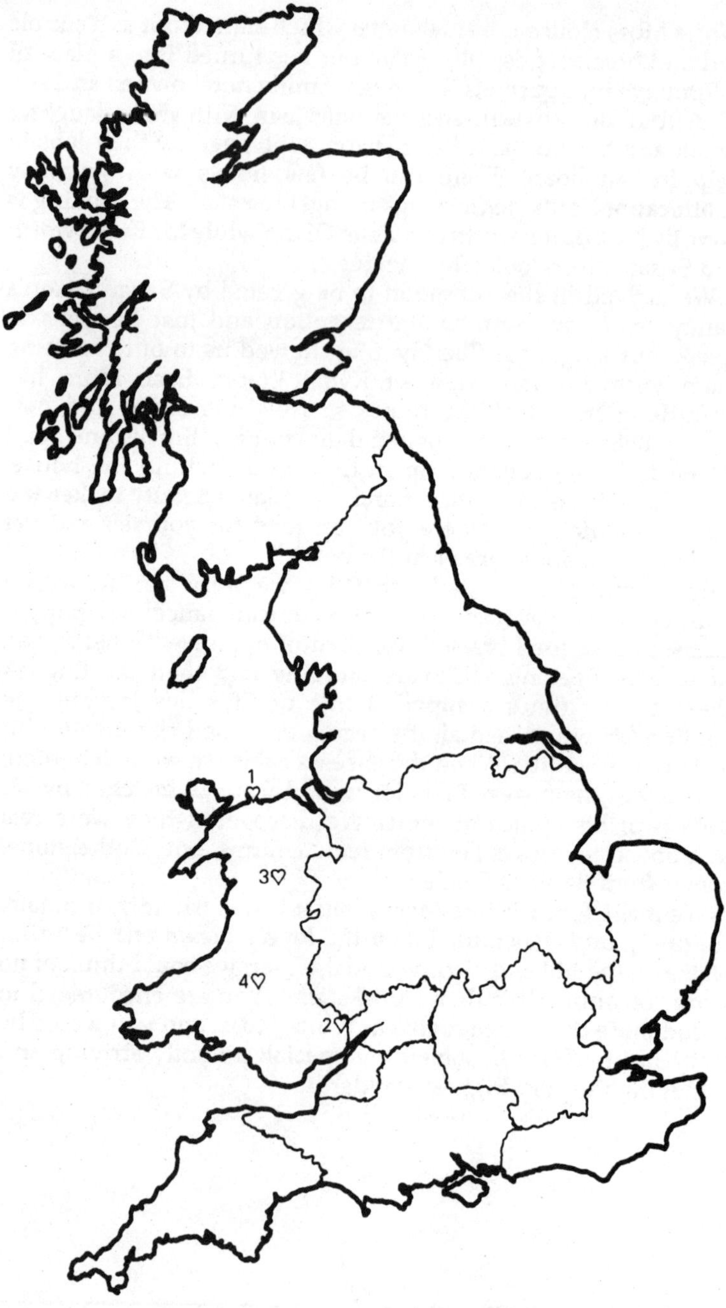
1
3
4
2

Wales

1 Bodysgallen Hall Hotel, Llandudno, Gwynedd
2 The Crown Inn, Whitebrook, Gwent
3 Lake Vyrnwy, Llanwddyn, Salop
4 Llwynderw, Abergwesyn, Powys

Bodysgallen Hall

Bodysgallen Hall Hotel
Llandudno
Gwynedd
North Wales
LL30 1RS
Tel: Deganwy (0492) 84466

Owner: Historic House Hotels
Resident Director: Nicholas Crawley
Cards: All
19 rooms, 9 cottage suites (all doubles or twins)
Dinner: 7.30–9.00
Lunch: 12.30–2.00
Breakfast: 8.00–9.30 (Sun till 10.00).
Early morning tea and papers in price.
English only in dining room

Children: Not under 8
Dogs: No
Closed: First week in February
Directions: Llandudno Junction (by the bridge to Conway) take the A 546 towards Llandudno. Take first right B5115 uphill. Bodysgallen is 1 mile on right hand side
Special Features: Historic house; Lovely gardens; Croquet
Price: ££

HOTEL: Buildings♥ Rooms♥ Food♡ Wine♡ Garden♥ Views♥
AMENITIES: Tennis♥ Swimming♡ Fishing♡ Golf♡ Riding♡ Beach♡ Croquet♥ Walks♥

Getting to Bodysgallen means getting to know Wales – we drove down the Conwy Estuary past the famous gardens of Bodnant to find ourselves at the steps leading up to the front door of this 17th-century house built round the earlier watchtower for Conwy Castle. Do ask to look out from the roof of the tower to see the views and also to admire the gardens from a different perspective.

Perhaps what surprised us about Bodysgallen was the feeling of a mature family country house. The original oak panelling and pargetted plaster work in the hall and upper sitting room provide a warm environment enlivened by the portraits, still lifes and watercolours on the walls, and the comfortable sofas which beckon one beside the fire. The hotel belongs to a new group: Historic House Hotels. This is their first project, carried out under the direction of Nicholas Crawley with his mother's help on the interior design. They have produced that comfortable relaxed atmosphere a country house should possess. It is discreet yet seductive.

Our room, with its four-poster with cleverly contrived patterned hangings, also had nice touches, such as a French print of a young man seducing a maiden and a bathroom equipped with all brass Edwardian style fittings and a good nailbrush.

The gardens have been restored and now harbour romantic nooks and arbours for lovers to stroll to their pleasure. The knot garden has been restored, a cupid splatters water into a lily pond and the doves fan themselves in the dovecote on the wall of the tower.

Not only does the hotel have pretty rooms in the house but the outbuildings have been converted to produce what is termed 'the village': a group of little cottages with one to three bedrooms and a kitchenette. The same level of impeccable taste is maintained. We saw the roof going on the secluded honeymoon cottage; that too will be equipped with its golfing umbrella to enable the guests to walk over to dinner.

The menu is based on good English food using the best ingredients. The service is swift.

Overall, Bodysgallen must rank as one of our most romantic hotels. Others think so too: when we visited it was already well-booked six months ahead, having opened but 20 months previously.

The Crown

The Crown at Whitebrook
Whitebrook
Nr Monmouth
Gwent
NP5 4TX
Tel: Monmouth (0600) 860254

Owners: John and David Jackson

Cards: Access, Amex, Diners, Visa

8 rooms (5 double, 2 twins)

Dinner: 7.00–10.00
Lunch: 12.00–2.00
Breakfast: 8.30–9.30

Children: Accepted but no special meals prepared

Dogs: Allowed but not in restaurant

Open: Year-round

Directions: Take the A466 north from Chepstow through Tintern. Just before Bigsweir Bridge turn left to Whitebrook

Special Features: Beautiful approach road; Wye Valley /streams; Walks

Price: £

HOTEL: Food♡ Wine♡ Views♡
AMENITIES: Fishing♡ Golf♡ Riding♡ Walks♥

The Crown was started by John and David Jackson in 1979. They like to describe it as a 'traditional French restaurant with rooms in an old Welsh country inn.'

The Crown is located in the pretty Whitebrook Valley in the Tintern Forest that falls to the River Wye. Part of the inn dates from 1680 but it has been restored and enlarged recently. The beamed and comfortable dining room is the oldest and nicest part with its views across the Little Valley to the steeply rising woods beyond.

There are romantic walks to be taken through the woods and along the stream to the river – a large St Bernard dog may keep you company. The atmosphere is of solitude but without being too wild or inhospitable.

Salmon fishing can be arranged at £40.00 per day upwards, and there is good riding and golf within easy reach.

Serious efforts are made with food and wine with good results. If anything dishes are a little too complicated (certainly the menu descriptions are) but we ate well with a chicken in cream, yoghurt and tarragon sauce and a local lamb with pear, brioche and brandy farce. We particularly liked buckwheat pancakes with Gruyere, mushroom and ham in a sabayon as a starter.

The service is provided by helpful and friendly ladies. The wine list is worth studying with some good bargains in the '77s. Ask John or David for advice – although they are not the kind of characters who you will engage in lengthy conversations.

Rooms are small and plain and not a great deal of imagination has been applied to them but most do have sympathetic views across the Little Valley of the Whitebrook. Be aware that they have been converted and soundproofing is not their strong point.

The Crown is in a magnificent and romantic setting and will provide you with good food and wine and early evening romantic strolls.

Lake Vyrnwy Hotel

Lake Vyrnwy Hotel
Llanwddyn
via Oswestry
Salop
SY10 OLY
(note: Hotel is actually in Powys, Wales)
Tel: Llanwddyn (069173) 244

Owners: Mrs J. F. Moir and Lt Col Sir John Baynes

Cards: None

30 rooms (11 with private bath, 3 doubles, 6 twins)

Dinner: 7.30 winter, 8.00 summer

Children: Accepted (not under 3 years in dining room)

Dogs: Yes (kennels) or outside but not in hotel

Directions: Take the A490 north from Welshpool to Llanfyllin, then the B4393 to Llanwddyn and Lake Vyrnwy

Special Features: Exclusive trout fishing on lake; Shooting; Music events

Price: £

HOTEL: Buildings♡ Rooms♡ Wine♡ Garden♡ Views♥
AMENITIES: Tennis♥ Fishing♥ Golf♡ Riding♡ Walks♥

Lake Vyrnwy Hotel is a truly old-fashioned sporting hotel which makes few concessions to be modern and none at all to look it. Almost everything is captivatingly original – the downstairs toilets must be seen! – and fortunately valued by its owners Mrs Moir and Lt Col Sir John Baynes. But don't worry, there is central heating. It sits high on a hill giving all the public rooms and lots of the bedrooms a superb panorama over the vast Lake Vyrnwy surrounded by wooded hillsides. This is a majestically peaceful and relaxing view in all weathers.

The rooms are simple with basic solid furniture. Only 11 have private baths and only seven have double beds – so book carefully.

The large dining room is set with solid white tablecloths and old hotel silver plate. Guests keep their serviettes in little 'porte serviettes' and dinner is served only at 8 (7.30 in winter!). The food itself is simple English country-house style, using good basic ingredients and the wine list is not over-long but contains some excellent wines at extremely good prices.

The Hotel controls all the trout fishing on the lake. Guests can borrow boats. In the winter the Hotel is the base for shooting on the 16,000-acre estate.

The area is superb for walking. There are gentle strolls along the lakeside road and paths as well as unlimited scope in the hills. The hotel has prepared illustrated guides to some interesting walks and you can borrow these to take with you. The whole estate is a bird conservation area. Riding is easily arranged nearby and bicycles can be rented for rides around the lake. Occasional concert events are arranged in the large sitting-room.

Whether you take part in all this activity or just use it as a backdrop for your other activities, Lake Vyrnwy is just the place for that old-fashioned romantic weekend. You will feel comfortable, relaxed and welcome.

After all the fresh air, cuddle up in the big leather armchairs in the little bar. Toast your toes on the wood-burning stove and tell each other romantic stories about your country childhood where it was just like this . . . open a nice bottle of wine . . . and if that doesn't work, you can always read the fishing magazines.

Lake Vyrnwy is a very welcome, old-fashioned treat.

Llwynderw

Llwynderw
Abergwesyn
Llanwrtyd Wells
Powys LD5 4TW
Tel: Llanwrtyd Wells (05913) 238

Resident owner: Michael Yates

Cards: none

10 rooms (7 doubles)

Dinner: 8.00 approx (when it's prepared!)
Lunch: 1.00, by request
Breakfast: 8.30–9.15

Children: Inadvisable

Dogs: By appointment

Closed: 1 November–1 April

Directions: From Builth Wells take the A483 to Beulah and Llanwrtyd Wells. Turn right on to the Abergwesyn road

Special Features: Isolated position; 'Specialized in doing nothing'; Atmosphere

Price: ££

HOTEL: Buildings♡ Rooms♥ Food♥ Wine♡ Views♡
AMENITIES: Fishing♡ Riding♡ Walks♥

Llwynderw is a very special, small hotel. Its quite remote location and unpronounceable name should continue to ensure that it is not too frequently visited! Don't try to reach it via Abergwesyn – the bridge has been down for some years and there is little prospect of its being repaired. Actually, you could try calling it 'Loo-in-derr-oo' according to the owner Michael Yates – but then he already knows where it is.

Mr Yates is absolutely charming and so is the little hotel he has owned for 15 years. The intimate sitting room, small library and 'Palm Court' are delightfully comfortable and relaxing. You will feel at home within five minutes as you sink into a comfortable armchair to read the local history collection that Mr Yates has assembled. The wall clock pendulum is the nearest anything comes to an interruption. A young man will bring you a drink on a silver tray. At most a handful of other guests will wander through – lulled like you into a state of peaceful relaxation, confident that this is the real world and everybody is wonderful. The rooms are all adorable. The views from the front are over trees to the forested hills beyond. There are one or two little gems amongst the artwork decorating the house which are all Mr Yates's personal items collected over the years.

Mr Yates supervises the cuisine and dinner is served when it's ready. The little dining room has small refectory-like tables and candlelight. The fixed daily menu is of a high quality. We enjoyed an excellent meal of coquille St Jacques, turnip soup, beef with beautifully cooked vegetables and followed by a good old-fashioned, proper green salad (why don't more people do it?). More is offered of every course. There is a very decent wine list with perhaps a little bit of a gap in the number of wines at £8–12.00 but nothing to worry about. You can help yourself to excellent coffee in the sitting rooms after dinner and chat to Mr Yates or his other guests, or you can browse through his interesting bookshelves. Later, when everyone has retired, this is the place for a quiet romantic chat on the sofa or perhaps a late-night backgammon session – board thoughtfully provided.

Llwynderw is a delight. You will return feeling refreshed.

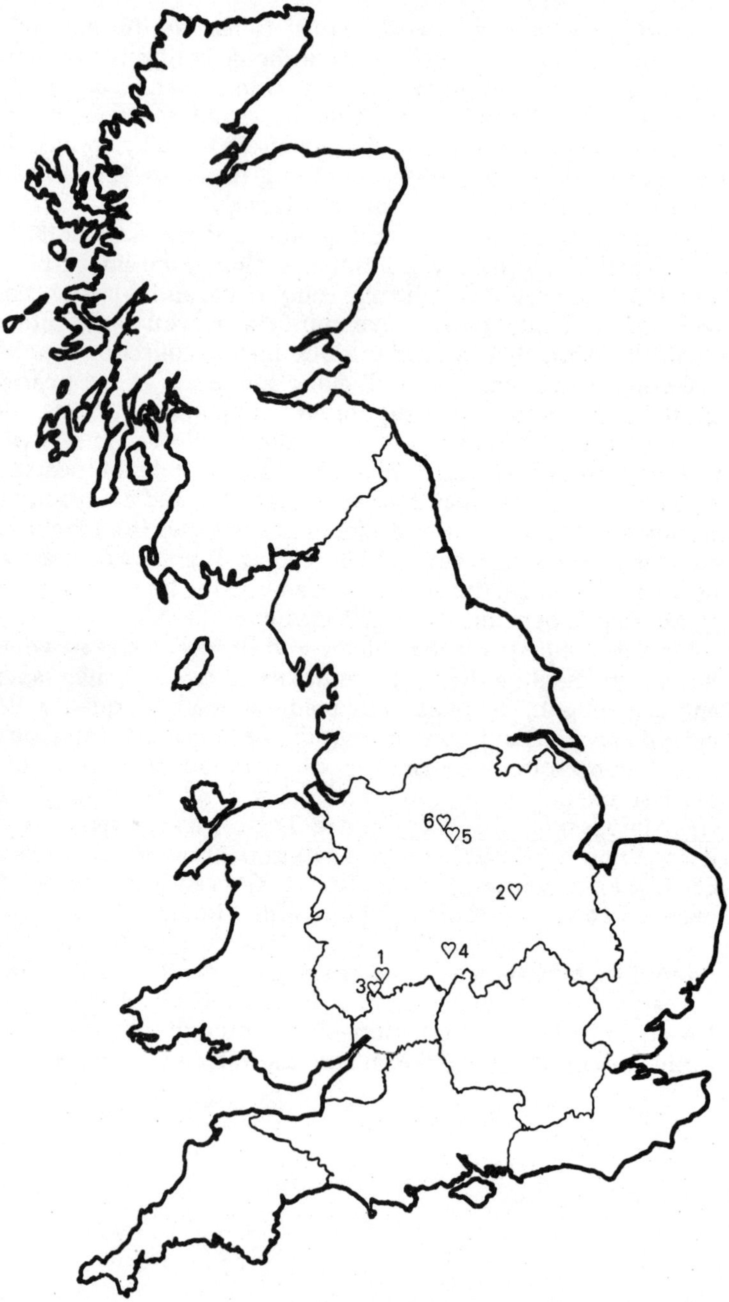
6
5
2
1
4
3

Central England

1 The Cottage in the Wood, Malvern, Worcestershire
2 Hambleton Hall, nr. Oakham, Leicestershire
3 Hope End Country House, Ledbury, Hereford
4 Mallory Court, Bishops Tachbrook, Warwickshire
5 Riber Hall, Matlock, Derby
6 Riverside Country House Hotel, Ashford-in-the-Water, Derby

The Cottage in the Wood

The Cottage in the Wood
Holywell Road
Malvern Wells
Worcs
WR14 4LG
Tel: Malvern (06845) 3487

Owner: Michael and Ellen Ross

Cards: Access, Visa

21 rooms (13 doubles, 8 twins, all with bathrooms)

Dinner: 7.15–9.00
Lunch: 12.30–2.00
Breakfast: 8.00–9.30 Continental (earlier by arrangement)

Children: Yes, but no special catering

Dogs: No

Open: Year-round

Directions: From Malvern take the A449 towards Ledbury. Look for hotel sign on the right and turn right into Holywell Road.

Special Features: One four-poster bed; Malvern Hills; Elgar Festival

Price: ££

HOTEL: Buildings♥ Rooms♡ Garden♡ Views♥
AMENITIES: Tennis♡ Fishing♡ Golf♡ Riding♡ Walks♥

The Cottage in the Wood nestles on the side of the Malvern Hills amongst the wonderful rhododendron-filled woods. The main building is a charming Georgian house containing nine suitably romantic (one beautiful four-poster) bedrooms and public rooms. These consist of a charming and welcoming red bar with open fire and, on the front of the house enjoying the spectacular views, the elegantly proportioned comfortable lounge and the attractive dining room. Other rooms are situated in two separate small cottages but all are delightfully individually decorated and share the expansive views. Marvellous walks can be taken up the winding footpaths through the woods. Owner Michael Ross achieves a relaxed and friendly atmosphere and is keen to help guests really enjoy the delights of the Malvern area. There are small lawned patios in front of the house and you can take your breakfast there to fully appreciate the Malvern experience on a summer morning.

Chef Graham Flanagan was not there the night we stayed so we found it difficult to comment fairly on the food (i.e. we had one or two quibbles!). However, the English cheeseboard was a pleasure and it is clear that successful efforts are being made to obtain the best of the small production of the English cheese renaissance. The single Gloucester and the Somerset brie were wonderful. The syllabub dessert was also excellent.

The Malvern area offers plenty of romantic things to do. The annual festival is now active again and theatre and music lovers will enjoy a stay in May. Nigel Kennedy was staying at the Cottage whilst we were there and the sweet strains of his Stradivarius occasionally wafted across the lawns! The 50th anniversary of Elgar's death will be in 1984 (he is buried nearby), so the Festival will be even more than usually Elgar-orientated.

Michael and Ellen Ross live at nearby Ledbury in The Grove, an old farmhouse with orchards and horses. If you ask nicely, Ellen Ross will let you stay in one of the rooms with four-poster beds (and private bath) and enjoy her cooking. This will cost you about £36.00 for two, including dinner and breakfast. Tel: Bromesberrow (053 181) 584.

Whilst in the area be sure to arrange a meal at the Croque en Bouche – one of our favourites.

Hambleton Hall

Hambleton Hall
Hambleton
Oakham
Rutland
LE15 8TH
Tel: Oakham (0572) 56991
Telex: 341995 Ref 207

Proprietors: Tim and Stefa Hart

Cards: AMX, Visa, Diners, Access

15 rooms (all doubles)

Dinner: 7.30–9.30
Lunch: 12.00–1.30
Breakfast: 7.30–9.30, English available in rooms (recommended)

Children: None under 9

Dogs: By arrangement

Open: Year-round

Directions: From the A1 at Stamford take the A606 to Oakham. When you reach Rutland Water look out for the badly marked turning on your left signposted Egleton and Hambleton village only. The hotel is in the middle of the peninsula

Special Features: Exceptional cuisine; Superb views; Beautiful rooms

Price: £££

HOTEL: Buildings♡ Rooms♥ Food♥ Wine♥ Garden♥ Views♥
AMENITIES: Tennis♥ Fishing♡ Golf♡ Riding♡ Sailing♡

You come to Hambleton Hall through pretty rolling countryside with stone villages reminiscent of the Cotswolds. Arriving beside Rutland Water you drive on to the peninsula stretching right into the middle of the lake. Here is the quiet village of Upper Hambleton and the hotel. Two lead cherubs cavort by the front door with its motto over it: 'Fay Ce Que Voudras' ('Do as you like'). With this admonishment in mind, this is the place for romance.

Most of the rooms, superbly decorated by Nina Campbell, look out over the water. We stayed in Middlehurst, done out in blue and buff with a glazed chintz canopy over the head of the bed and beside it a tin masquerading as a cottage filled with heart-shaped biscuits. The room has a cool, serene elegance, some fresh flowers from the garden are matched by a pyramid of dried ones on the chest of drawers. Even the spacious bathroom shares the breathtaking view. For pure magnificence choose 'Qazvin' decorated by Stefa Hart in sumptuous Turkish splendour with an amazing domed bed and sofa.

Flowers are everywhere, with banks of flowers cascading down from the terrace to huge scented arrangements inside the house. These provide the setting for one of England's most creative chefs, Nicholas Gill, to seduce you with his cuisine. The menu is presented on a card folded to give six sides with a little vignette over each page: the first course, second, main, cheese, sweet and specials of the day. Each course has a choice of three to five dishes where you may choose a simple but perfect meal or go for something more adventurous. We always go for the adventurous and had a marinade of fresh salmon with limes and coriander; a soufflé of fresh sea urchins (served in the shell); sirloin of beef; some superb cheeses, well presented by the waiters, and an iced raspberry soufflé.

Tim Hart has a wonderful sense of humour (read his 'Things to do around Hambleton Hall'). In our opinion he has achieved the perfect balance for an hotel: personality, beauty, great food and superb service which is discreet yet friendly, and all in a wonderful setting. Need we say more?

Hope End

Hope End Country House Hotel
Hope End
Ledbury
Hereford
HR8 IJQ
Tel: Ledbury (0531) 3613

Resident Owners: John and Patricia Hegarty

Cards: All

7 rooms (1 double, 6 twins)

Dinner: 7.30–9.00
Lunch: Not served
Breakfast: 8.30–9.30

Children: No

Dogs: No

Closed: December–mid-February

Directions: From Ledbury take Broomyard direction and turn right after going under railway bridge to Wellington Heath. Follow winding lane for 1½ miles to T-junction at top of hill. Turn right to fork. Bear right to pass Hope End Farm on right. Hope End is on left

Special Features: Room with minaret!; Childhood home of Elizabeth Barrett Browning; Malvern Hills; Good food

Price: ££

HOTEL: Buildings♥ Rooms♥ Food♥ Wine♥ Garden/Grounds♥ Views♥
AMENITIES: Walks♥

Arriving at Hope End is more like visiting your nice country relatives than staying at an hotel. Entering the courtyard you might find nobody about, but you will doubtless detect the wonderful aroma of well-conducted culinary activities.

Hope End is owned and run by Patricia and John Hegarty and is a truly romantic country house. It is not grand but comfortable and of top quality. The building was once part of the childhood home of Elizabeth Barrett Browning (how romantic can you get?). The hotel consists of only seven rooms. A pretty upstairs lounge with log fires and a little collection of the history of the house overlooks some of the 40 acres of grounds. The small dining room is, if anything, a little too intimate – not the place for a big seduction scene! The whole house is adorned with original and tasteful paintings, drawings and ornaments.

All of the rooms are attractive and have private bathrooms. Those in the main building have twin beds, however, so if your idea of a romantic weekend necessitates a double bed, you must stay in the 'romantic room'. This is in its own little wing just across the courtyard and under the minaret. It is intimate, comfortable, warm and unpretentious. The sun comes into the bathroom in the morning and you will look out over the parkland down towards the ponds. There are no TVs, telephones or any other intrusions, just scented bath oils, a darning box and thimble and a large umbrella!

Patricia's cooking is excellent. It is sophisticated beyond the English misconception that good food equals rich and complex sauces. She cooks simply, with imagination and superb ingredients. Local meat and fish are at their best in this part of the country and the tasty vegetables (including sorrel and sea kale) and fruit come from the Hegartys' own walled garden. Goat's milk adds a lightness to simple sauces and produces an excellent yoghurt.

Patricia prepares a different menu every day and bakes her own bread. Great interest is taken in English cheeses and serious efforts made always to have something interesting; the Belvoir Blue was magnificent. The wine list is a pleasure with a good range of interesting and sensible wines and some excellent bargains. John will advise if necessary.

The beautiful grounds are well-wooded and set in extensive countryside. Early risers can chase the rabbits, spot the birds and identify the flowers on their walks through the hills. The wider area is outstandingly attractive with several small market towns and villages and the Malvern Hills to be explored. Do go.

Mallory Court

Mallory Court
Harbury Lane
Bishop's Tachbrook
Leamington Spa
Warks
CV33 9QB
Tel: Leamington Spa (0926) 30214

Owners: Allan Holland and Jeremy Mort

Cards: Access, Visa, American Express

10 rooms (5–6 double, 2–3 twin, 1 suite and 1 four-poster)

Dinner: 7.30–9.45 (after-theatre supper can be supplied if ordered in advance)

Lunch: 12.30–1.45
Breakfast: 7.30–10
Children: Over 12

Dogs: No

Open: Year-round

Directions: Follow signs for Harbury off A452 between Bishop's Tachbrook and Leamington Spa

Special Features: Near Stratford and other places of interest; Wonderful food

Price: £££

HOTEL: Buildings♡ Rooms♥ Food♥ Wine♥ Garden♥ Views♡
AMENITIES: Swimming♥ Golf♡ Croquet♥ Walks♡

A sense of discreet opulence greeted us at Mallory Court, built in the style of Lutyens, with tall brick chimneys and diamond-paned windows. The armchairs by the fire in the hall are deep and comfortable; indeed, guests are nurtured and cossetted in every way. Jeremy Mort has exquisite taste and all the bedrooms are delectable. Using the original 1930s bathroom fittings, he has cleverly made use of space so that each bedroom has its own delightful bathroom (the 'Blenheim Suite' even has twin baths) with scented soap, shampoo and bath oils, and large fluffy bathrobes. Every possible wish has been anticipated.

Delicious smells tempted us to the oak-panelled dining room where Jeremy Mort's elegant touch is just as noticeable. Spacious tables are laid with pale green linen and courteous waiters tread noiselessly on deep pile carpets as they serve faultlessly-presented nouvelle cuisine, excellently cooked by Allan Holland, whose dishes are complex and inventive without being fussy, accompanied by well-chosen wines. Or you might prefer to see a Shakespeare play at nearby Stratford and have an intimate after-theatre supper.

Waking refreshed in our pretty room, we enjoyed a delicious breakfast of homemade croissants, local honey and a large cafetière of excellent coffee – if only more hotels would follow suit! Strolling in the flower-filled gardens, lazing on the swing seat or splashing in the 1930s pool, the realities of everyday life are far away. Mallory Court gives a glimpse of a golden age when elegant prosperity reigned supreme.

Riber Hall

Riber Hall
Matlock
Derby
DE4 5JU
Tel: Matlock (0629) 2795 and 3730

Owner: Alex Biggin

11 rooms (all doubles, 10 with four-posters)

Cards: All

Dinner: 7–9.30
Breakfast: 7 (8 on Sun) – 9.30
Lunch: 12–1.30 (packed lunches available)

Children: No

Dogs: No

Open: Year-round

Directions: Follow signs for Riber off A615 at Tansley (the hotel is *near*, not in, Matlock)

Special Features: Good centre for visiting stately homes

Price: ££

HOTEL: Buildings♡ Rooms♡ Food♡ Wine♡ Garden♥
AMENITIES: Walks♡

The fragrant scent of jasmine greeted us as we entered the conservatory where the reception desk of Riber Hall is discreetly concealed. Fifteen years ago this Elizabethan manor house was virtually derelict. Alex Biggin carefully restored it, first opening a restaurant and then cleverly converting the barn across the courtyard to provide atmospheric bedrooms with four-poster beds and beamed ceilings. Indeed, in one bedroom the beams are so low that it proved impossible to squeeze in a four-poster, but there is a carved antique bedhead instead.

Sherry, chocolate and fruit are thoughtfully placed on the bedside table with the compliments of the owners, who also provide Roger & Gallet soaps, shampoo, bubblebath and soap flakes in the pretty bathrooms. If you need further sustenance, a refrigerated bar is provided in each room.

Wander back across the courtyard to the small bar furnished with Jacobean antiques to choose from the wide-ranging menu (making good use of local game and fish when in season) and the carefully selected wine list. There are two intimate, candle-lit dining rooms, where silver and polished wood gleam; service is friendly and informal without being obtrusive.

Next morning, after a delicious breakfast of homemade croissants and jam, enjoy the pretty gardens which are tended by Alex Biggin's delightful mother, who also makes all the hangings and patchwork quilts for the four-poster beds. Indeed, Riber Hall is very much a family hotel as Alex's wife also devotes her energies to making one's stay supremely pleasant.

Friendly and caring as the Biggins and their staff are, you won't feel overwhelmed by their attentions. This lovely house is hard to beat as the setting for a secluded romance.

Riverside Country House Hotel

Riverside Country House Hotel
Ashford-in-the-Water
Nr Bakewell
Derby
Tel: Bakewell (062 981) 4275

Owners: Susan and Roger Taylor

Cards: Access, Visa, American Express

4 rooms (all doubles)

Dinner: 7.30–9.30
Lunch: Bar lunch, 12.30–2.30 weekdays; full lunch 1 on Sun
Breakfast: By arrangement

Open: Year-round

Children: Welcome

Dogs: Welcome

Directions: On A6 between Bakewell and Buxton

Special Features: Good centre for exploring Derby Peaks and visiting stately homes

Price: £

HOTEL: Wine♡ Garden♡
AMENITIES: Croquet♥ Walks♡

The charming village of Ashford is in the heart of the Peak District and here Sue and Roger Taylor have opened their small, restful hotel. The attractive house, built by one of the Dukes of Devonshire, stands in a walled garden and borders the River Wye. A friendly dog and cat watch over the front door. There are only four rooms, each with a bath en suite, all prettily decorated by Sue Taylor. They are comfortable and airy but, understandably, are not equipped with all the extra luxuries that more expensive hotels offer.

While Roger Taylor prepares dinner, Sue serves drinks in the small bar. The set menu, which is frequently changed, offers remarkable value: a five-course meal for no more than many restaurants charge for a main course alone. Ingredients are fresh and portions are generous – just what is needed after a day exploring Chatsworth and the other nearby great houses in this little-known but extremely beautiful part of England. This really is a place to get away from it all, wandering in the unspoilt countryside around Ashford or simply lazing in the pleasant garden. It's very much like staying with friends. You won't be pampered and pandered to as in a larger, more glamorous establishment, but you will find intimacy, tranquillity and exceptionally good value.

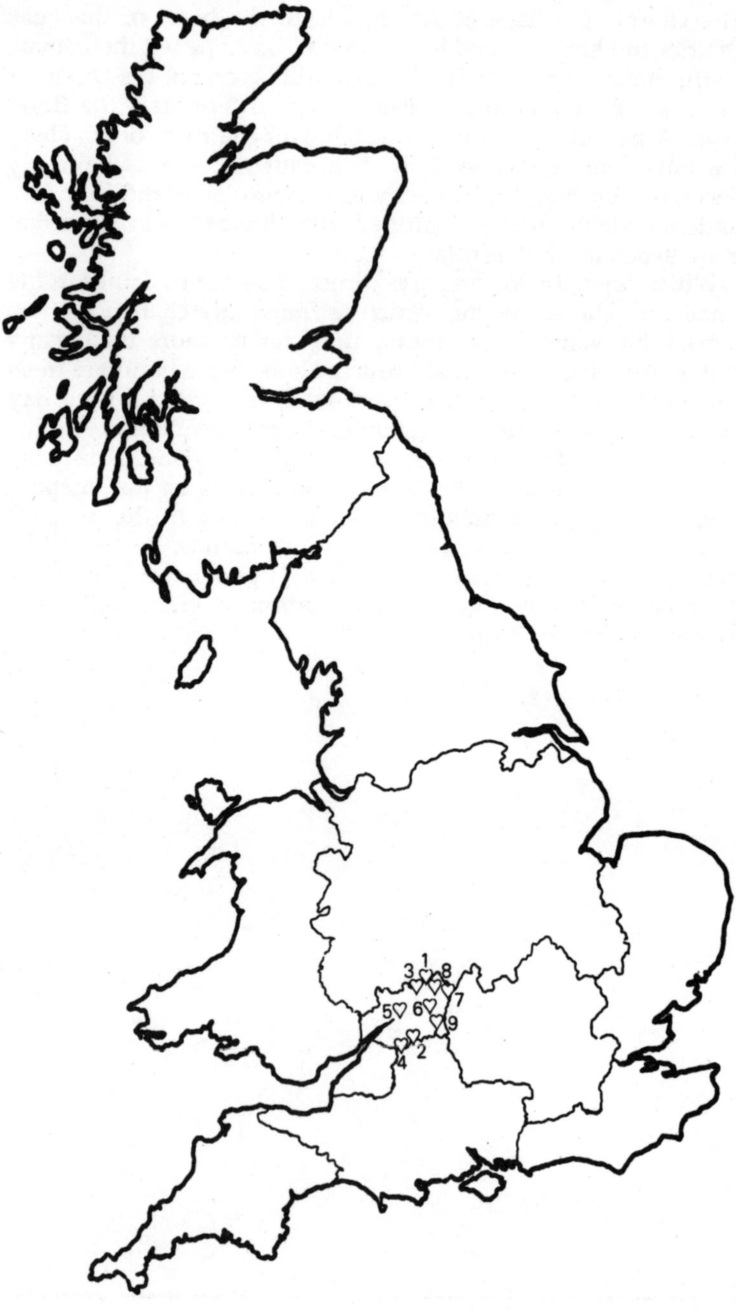
1
2
3
4
5
6
7
8
9

The Cotswolds

1 Buckland Manor, Broadway, Worcestershire
2 The Close, Tetbury, Gloucestershire
3 Dormy House, Broadway, Worcestershire
4 The Gentle Gardener, Tetbury, Gloucestershire
5 The Greenway, Shurdington, Gloucestershire
6 Lords of the Manor Hotel, Upper Slaughter, Gloucestershire
7 Lower Brook House, Blockley, Worcestershire
8 The Lygon Arms, Broadway, Worcestershire
9 The Swan, Bibury, Gloucestershire

Buckland Manor

Buckland Manor
Buckland
Glos WR12 7LY
Tel: Broadway (0386) 852626

Owners: Barry and Adrienne Berman

Cards: Access, Visa, American Express, Diners

11 rooms (all double with baths en suite, 3 with additional separate showers, two four-posters)

Dinner: 7.00–9.30
Lunch: 12.00–2.00
(times may be varied by arrangement)
Breakfast: 8.00–10.30

Children: None under 12
Dogs: Not allowed (kennels available within the grounds)

Open: Year-round

Directions: Follow signs to Buckland off A46 between Broadway and Cheltenham

Special Features: Good centre for walking and exploring Cotswolds

Price: £££

HOTEL: Buildings♥ Rooms♥ Food♡ Wine♡ Garden♥ Views♥
AMENITIES: Tennis♥ Swimming♥ Golf♡ Riding♡ Croquet♥ Walks♥

Barry and Adrienne Berman have achieved something many people dream of doing: having raised their family, they have undergone a complete change of lifestyle and are now the proud owners of a handsome Cotswold manor house which, moreover, they renovated, redecorated and furnished beautifully in a remarkably short time. They are to be congratulated on the peace, comfort and beauty which pervades this fine house. Elegant furniture is arranged round a blazing log fire in the beamed and panelled sitting room where drinks are served. Exquisite ornaments and pictures are everywhere; beyond the house lie well-tended gardens and fields of sheep and horses.

The menu, served in the white-panelled dining room, is elaborate. All ingredients are fresh, the dishes varied and complex. The wine list has been stocked with a good range of bottles to suit all tastes. The Bermans have taken immense trouble with detail here as everywhere: plates are hot, coffee is served in a cafetière (if only more hotels would follow that practice), fresh flowers are everywhere. Meals and drinks can also be served outdoors on the terrace or in the gardens overlooking the croquet lawn.

Malvern water and bowls of fruit are placed in all bedrooms, which are prettily furnished and decorated and contain everything one could need for a pleasant stay. The proportion of staff to guests is high, as are the prices, but quality of this kind does not come cheaply.

Buckland is a very pretty village, close to Broadway and other Cotswold attractions, yet quiet and away from the tourist track. Next to the Manor is a 13th-century church with an unusual medieval painted ceiling, recently discovered. There is plenty to do in and around the hotel – explore the beautiful gardens, swim in the heated pool, play tennis or golf, ride in the lovely countryside – or curl up by the fire with a book if it's raining.

The Bermans have really thrown themselves into the art of running a fine country house hotel, and we hope they will soon be able to relax and enjoy the environment they have so skilfully created.

The Close at Tetbury

The Close at Tetbury
8 Long Street
Tetbury
Glos GL8 8AQ
Tel: Tetbury (0666) 52272
Telex: 43232 Ref CLH

Managing Director: J. M. Lauzier

Cards: All (cheques preferred)

12 rooms: (6 doubles, 1 four-poster, 3 twins)

Dinner: 7.30–9.45
Lunch: 12.30–1.45
Breakfast: 7.00–10.00 in rooms
English 8.00–9.30 in dining room only

Children: Welcome

Dogs: No
Closed: First week in January
Special Features: Doves; Garden; Pretty village
Price: ££ (special weekend rates)

HOTEL: Buildings♡ Food♥ Wine♡ Garden♡
AMENITIES: Tennis♡ Golf♡ Riding♡ Croquet♥

More than a hint of Continental hospitality can be found at this charming small hotel, set in the heart of picturesque Tetbury – the Cotswold market-town famed most recently for its nearby Royal residence. Run by Jean-Marie Lauzier, considerate and courteous service is the hallmark of the Close, where you will be impressed by the friendly, efficient staff, for whom nothing is too much trouble. There are six double rooms (one with a four-poster) and three twin-bedded rooms, all attractively and simply decorated in keeping with the character of the hotel. I was particularly aware of the enormously detailed attention which had been given to my room, including flowers, mineral water and – which was sorely needed after a long, hot car journey – a trouser press. In the bathroom every sort of toiletry and helpful accessory was to be found, down to a hairdryer, nail scissors and a needle and cotton!

The beautiful warm summer evening gave us the opportunity to sit under a parasol drinking delicious Pimms in the quiet enclosed garden. The giant lime trees cast their dappled green shade and the doves cooed and fluttered in and out of the dovecote high up on the wall of the hotel. The spirit of the evening was continued by a delectable dinner, which we chose with difficulty from a tempting (but not vast) menu of unusual dishes. I shall remember with particular pleasure a superb, delicate fish paté served warm with a butter sauce – quite excellent without being too rich or filling. Another option that we noted was 'Caneton aux Kumquats' which, through ignorance and lacking the courage to ask, we decided against! We could have had a French regional menu – which changes every month. Meanwhile, the wine list, with many good wines, was very reasonably priced.

After a comfortable night and a welcome, very hot, bath, down to an old-fashioned English breakfast for which I chose local rainbow trout, which melted in the mouth, washed down by limitless quantities of excellent coffee. All in all, it is a haven of peace and comfort with a great deal to recommend it, not least that it is extremely competitively priced for a hotel of its quality. One small word of warning – make sure you ask for larger bath towels and robes than the rather conservative ones provided – after the food you will have consumed, they will certainly be needed!

Dormy House

Dormy House
Willersey Hill
Broadway
Worcs WR12 7LF
Tel: Broadway (0386) 852711
Telex: 338571

General Manager: Harvey Pascoe

Cards: All

50 rooms (3 suites, 10 doubles plus 2 four-posters, all with bathrooms en suite)

Dinner: 7.30–10.00
Breakfast: 7.30–10.00
Lunch: 12.30–2.00

Children: Allowed

Dogs: Allowed except in public rooms

Open: Year round

Directions: Discreetly marked turning (on right when approaching from Oxford) off A44 (Broadway Hill). Golf club shares same turning. The hotel is *not* in Broadway or Willersey – the address is confusing.

Special features: Good area for Cotswold sightseeing; Squash; Clay pigeon-shooting by arrangement

Price: ££/£££

HOTEL: Buildings♡ Rooms♥ Food♥ Wine♥ Garden♡ Views♥
AMENITIES: Tennis♡ Golf♡ Riding♡ Walks♥

The motto of Dormy House is 'Vigilamus dum dormitis' ('We guard while you sleep') and, under the enthusiastic management of Harvey Pascoe, the hotel lives up to this maxim. His zest is infectious and all the staff share his affability and courtesy; everyone obviously enjoys working there. The atmosphere is relaxed without being over-casual.

The 17th-century farm buildings have been so tastefully converted and extended that it's hard to tell which are original and which are new. Our room had its own entrance from the garden, enhancing the sense of privacy, and was thoughtfully equipped with all the essentials for a pleasant stay. The decor stylishly blended fabrics and colours which took their keynote from the warm Cotswold stone. We immediately felt soothed and well-cared for, forgetting the pressures of work as the calmness of the countryside lulled and relaxed us.

Each room has its own character and charm with skilful arrangements of dried and fresh flowers, attractive pictures and unusually good lighting (there is even a spotlight over the bath!), all selected by the talented Danish wife of the owner.

Before dinner we had drinks in one of the intimate nooks and corners that fill the maze of small rooms in the original farmhouse.

Presiding over the kitchens is the distinguished-looking maître chef, Roger Chant, who has worked with Paul Bocuse and the Troisgros brothers, as we could tell from the beautiful presentation of the delicious food prepared from the finest ingredients. He has fish brought fresh from Cornwall, meat aged to perfection, seasonings blended by Roger Vergé and specially imported – paradise for gourmets like us. The wines are well-chosen and include an excellent house wine.

We woke to the sound of bird-song and spent a lazy morning strolling on the golf course which surrounds the hotel and admiring the landscape spread below, then had lunch in the Cotswold Bar where the menu is chalked up each day by a highly artistic bartender. Later we drove to Hidcote, that exquisite secret garden, one of the many beautiful houses and gardens nearby.

The Gentle Gardener

The Gentle Gardener
Long Street
Tetbury
Glos
Tel: Tetbury (0666) 52884

Owners/Managers: Judy and Warren Knock

Cards: Visa/Diners

5 rooms (3 doubles, 1 with double bed; 2 singles)

Open: Year-round

Restaurant open: Wed–Sat, but residents catered for (smaller menu)

Children: Welcome

Dogs: By arrangement

Dinner: 7.30–10
Lunch: Bar lunch 12.00–2.15
Breakfast: 7.30–9.30 English breakfast in dining room only

Special Features: Stone-walled garden; Very attractive dining room; Westonbirt Arboretum nearby

Price: £ (special rates available)

HOTEL: Food♡ Wine♡ Garden♡

When we discovered that there was a place called The Gentle Gardener, we had to visit it. We found a small, old hotel with a stone-walled garden which has been lovingly restored after years of neglect by the gentle gardeners Judy and Warren Knock, who have recently acquired the place. The garden makes an ideal spot to sip a beer or drowse after lunch beneath the ancient apple trees. The old Victorian roses and herbs scent the air on hot summer days whilst entertainment can be had from watching or participating in a game of old-fashioned skittles.

Judy and Warren Knock previously owned a restaurant in Tooting, and with help from local staff they run a friendly and unpretentious hotel. There are only five rooms, none yet with their own bathroom but all adequately comfortable though a little noisy in the morning from the Long Street traffic. We had fresh fruit, flowers, books and magazines in our room. Nice touches in a simple unpretentious place which show the Knocks' concern to look after their guests.

The evening menu can be discussed with Warren Knock while you sample the local Archers or Cirencester bitter in the bar with its open fire. The dining room then comes as a lovely surprise: seating 26 it is beautifully and originally decorated with its stripped polished oak floor, yellow walls and tablecloths and blue covered chairs. There are spectacular arrangements of dried flowers and old garden implements with painted buckets hanging from the ceiling which makes it an especially attractive and interesting room, and a great subject for conversation during dinner.

The food is prepared by Judy Knock and could be described as excellent English food with creative touches. To start we had the 'Hot Fish Terrine', a turbot and salmon terrine with mushroom sauce. Then there were a choice of five main courses; we chose the 'Breast of Duck with Moutarde de Meaux' and the 'Beefsteak Champ de Mars', the latter being pan-fried and served with an excellent and subtle sauce of cream, Stilton and almonds. For pudding we chose the strawberry gateau and the chocolate marquis. The service was particularly discreet and friendly.

After a good English breakfast of grapefruit, bacon and eggs, toast and coffee a walk at the nearby Westonbirt Arboretum can be recommended. Here is another of those tiny hotels where a family is really trying; it's not smart but it's got style.

The Greenway

The Greenway
Shurdington
Cheltenham
Glos GL51 5UG
Tel: Cheltenham (0242) 862352
Telex: 437216

Owners: Tony and Maryan Elliott

Cards: All

12 rooms (3 doubles, one with half-tester bed)

Dinner: 7.30–9.30
Lunch: 12.30–2.00
Breakfast: 7.30–9.30

Children: None under 7

Dogs: No

Directions: On A46 2½ miles south of Cheltenham

Special Features: Historic house; Good centre for exploring Cotswolds and Vale of Evesham

Price: ££/£££

HOTEL: Buildings♥ Rooms♡ Food♡ Wine♡ Garden♥ Views♥
AMENITIES: Golf♡ Croquet♥ Walks♡

82

At the sumptuous Greenway, a staff of 18 tend a maximum of 22 guests. Cattle graze in the meadow in front of this 16th-century mansion where you'll be greeted by Bumble the cat and Hubble-Bubble, the cheerful little dog. In the hall large, comfortable chairs are ranged round one of the many splendid fireplaces. Oil paintings line the grand staircase that leads to the bedrooms.

The Greenway is a country house (though within easy reach of Cheltenham) and that is the style which the Elliotts have maintained. All the bedrooms, even the charming attic rooms, are large, furnished with antiques, and tastefully decorated. Many look out on to the beautifully tended gardens at the back and all are provided with those thoughtful extras, such as Malvern water, Floris soaps and bath gel, which contribute to making one's stay memorable. The atmosphere is tranquil; even when the hotel is full it's easy to find a quiet corner where one can sit undisturbed by the fire with a *very* good friend.

In the wood-panelled dining room, the fixed-price menu offers plenty of choice using only fresh produce. Fish is brought regularly from Wales and locally grown wild mushrooms are an unusual delicacy. Herbs and salads are grown in the hotel's own gardens by the perfectly named Mr Sowerbutts, Mrs Tempest and Basil.

Charming stone cherubs watch over the lily-pond and stone-flagged terrace where you can lunch off cold salmon and strawberries – the ultimate English summer treat. The Greenway is a haven of peace.

Lords of the Manor

Lords of the Manor Hotel
Upper Slaughter
Bourton-on-the-Water
Cheltenham
Glos
GL54 2JD
Tel: Bourton-on-the-Water (0451) 20243
Telex: via 83147 ref LORDS

Manager: Anthony de Trafford

Cards: Visa, Access, Diners, American Express

15 rooms (8 doubles, including 2 four-posters, all with private bath, most en suite)

Dinner: 7.30–9.30 (8.45 on Sun)

Lunch: 12.30–1.45 (full lunch), 12.30–2 (bar lunch)

Breakfast: 8–9.30 (weekdays) 8.30–10 (Sun)

Children: Allowed

Dogs: Not allowed in bedrooms (in any case, check first with manager)

Open: Year-round

Directions: Follow signs for Upper Slaughter (near Lower Slaughter) off A429 between Stow-on-the-Wold and Bourton-on-the-Water

Special Features: Attractive historic setting; Excellent trout fishing; Good base for exploring Cotswolds

Price: ££

HOTEL: Buildings♥ Rooms♥ Food♡ Wine♥ Garden♥ Views♥
AMENITIES: Fishing♥ Croquet♥ Walks♥

The 17th-century manor house is set in exceptionally pretty grounds. The Manor is still owned by the Witts family who have lived there for 200 years; family portraits and mementoes are everywhere and the rooms are named after families connected with the Witts through marriage.

When we arrived the bar was crowded; in an instant, Anthony de Trafford (who runs the hotel) had discerned that we were lovers in search of privacy and led us to the quiet, comfortable drawing room whose large windows have splendid views over green pastures, where cows graze picturesquely. The garden room, tucked away, is even more intimate and restful.

All of the bedrooms are comfortably furnished and most are large and airy. Pretty trays with Nina Campbell china and a selection of coffee and Jackson's tea are provided. Each room has an individual character and most have lovely views. No TV or radio is provided in the rooms, but TV addicts will find a large set in the garden room. Far more enjoyable, though, to fish for trout, play croquet, wander around the Cotswolds or read 'The Diary of a Country Parson', written by a 19th-century member of the Witts family.

The restaurant is surprisingly large but divided so that one isn't aware of its size; there are candles and flowers on every table. The food it not as stylish or inventive as some we have encountered, but the portions are immense, wholesome and filling – just what one needs after a day of country pursuits. Try the salmon locally smoked over oak chips. Order duck and half the bird spans your plate; the waitress seems amazed that you can't finish the large quantities of fresh vegetables. Restaurant prices are considerably lower than in most hotels of this standard; the wine list is varied and offers some exceptional burgundies.

In a country house hotel it's hard to strike the balance between providing the amenities one requires from a good hotel and the atmosphere of a lived-in house. We feel that the de Traffords have got it right. The Manor is neither overly formal nor overly casual; decoration and furnishing are well-planned but not overwhelming; the result is a relaxed and calming atmosphere, and exceptionally good value for money.

Lower Brook House

Lower Brook House
Blockley
Moreton-in-Marsh
Glos GL56 9DS
Tel: 0386 700286

Owner: Ewan Wright

Cards: Access

8 rooms (all with double beds, 7 with bathroom or shower)

Dinner: 7.30–9.00
Lunch: 12.30–1.45
Breakfast: 8.30–9.15

Children: Welcome

Dogs: By arrangement

Closed: Last 2 weeks of January

Directions: Take the A44 from Moreton-in-Marsh to Bourton-on-the-Hill. Turn right to Blockley

Special Features: Cotswold village

Price: £

HOTEL: Buildings♡ Food♡ Wine♡ Garden♡
AMENITIES: Golf♡ Riding♡ Walks♥

Lower Brook House is in the charming village of Blockley and has a small but attractive terraced garden with a view to the village church. The garden, where drinks and tea are served in summer, leads to a small brook after which the hotel is named.

The building is a typical Cotswold house. The ground floor consists of an attractive dining room and a wonderful oak-beamed lounge with flag stones, cosy sofas and the proverbial inglenook fireplace. There are great log fires in the winter whilst you sip your after-dinner port. This part of the building dates from the 17th century. Adjoining the lounge is a cosy little bar which usually has a few locals having a pint or two.

Guests are welcomed by Ewan Wright who now owns Lower Brook House after learning the hotel and catering business in various parts of the world, including The Norfolk in Nairobi. He and his young staff are making an effort to establish a good quality service. Above all, efforts will be made to make you feel relaxed. Guests, owner, staff and local characters rapidly seem to develop a friendly rapport.

The food is essentially traditional English (with a few embellishments), based on the excellent local produce of the Vale of Evesham. We enjoyed superb local lamb, good vegetables, including gratinée parsnips, good Stilton and Helen's homemade Paris Brest. Special efforts are made with local game in season. The service is efficient and friendly. The wine list is perfectly adequate with some very drinkable wines at £6–10.00.

The rooms vary greatly in what they have to offer. Most now have bathrooms, (one, a shower instead) and most have double beds. Soundproofing is not the strongest point so we suggest you say you are honeymooning when you reserve! Rooms 6, 7 and 8 are in the roof with sloping ceilings and number 4 is called the 'Honeymoon Room'.

The location offers a lot in the way of walks and local interest. You must take 'Walks for Motorists: Cotswolds, Northern Area' by Peter Price (Frederick Warne). The nearby market town of Chipping Campden is superb. Romantic weekenders will enjoy an arm-in-arm stroll through the nearby Batsford Arboretum. This is some 50 acres started by Lord Redesdale in the 1880s and since built up as a well maintained collection of trees and plants.

Lygon Arms

The Lygon Arms
The High Street
Broadway
Worcs WR12 7DU
Tel: Broadway (0386) 85 2255
Telex: 338260

Manager: Kirk Ritchie

Cards: All

67 rooms (33 doubles with 3 four-posters – Charles I, The Great Chamber and No. 8 – 4 rooms with gas log fires)

Breakfast: English and champagne (available in room)

Dinner: Till 9.30 (fireside, candlelight) Late dinners also available

Lunch: 12.30–1.45
Breakfast: 8.00–10.00 cooked, continental available earlier.

Children and dogs: Welcome

Open: Year-round

Special Features: 16th-century coaching inn; pretty village; Log fires and Great Hall

Price: £££

HOTEL: Buildings♥ Rooms♥ Food♥ Wine♥ Garden♡
AMENITIES: Tennis♥ Golf♡ Riding♡ Walks♡

You will be pampered with charm at the Lygon Arms. When we arrived my wife left one of her dresses in the car but the member of staff who parked it noticed it and brought it in for us. This sort of concern makes the Inn such a special place. They have been looking after guests for 450 years and the hotel still retains the feel of a coaching inn with oak panelling and blazing log fires. There are three rooms with four-posters.

We stayed in the Charles I suite with a magnificent four-poster, antique oak furniture and a fire; the sitting room en suite has its own fire too, lovely blue china and pewter plates and has a real parlour feel. The welcome in your room says it all: two glasses of sherry and savoury biscuits on a table, two bottles of Malvern water by your bed, not only bath towels but bathrobes in your bathroom. There really is nothing missing: a little jug of bubblebath, a bowl of Lux flakes along with a telephone and weighing scales. Honeymoon couples even get heart-shaped soaps!

Kirk Ritchie who runs the hotel is both charming and totally professional; in fact he visited the hotel at the age of 12 and decided to become the manager then and there. We dined with him and his wife, who spoiled us with a beautiful bottle of Leoville Barton '77 which was perfectly decanted and completed the excellent dinner cooked by Shaun Hill, one of the new breed of English chefs. It was creative but not too 'nouvelle cuisine'. Items from the à la carte menu are included in the set dinner menu which is changed daily. We had a 'Bouquet of Salads with Quail Eggs' and sweetbread beignets followed by 'Saddle of Lamb and Sorrel'.

Start the day with the champagne breakfast, and then visit the picturesque village of Broadway and the lovely Cotswold countryside all around.

The Swan Hotel

The Swan Hotel
Bibury
Glos
GL7 5NW
Tel: Bibury (0285 74) 204

Proprietor: Colin T. Morgan

Cards: All

24 rooms (9 doubles, 11 twins, nearly all with views over the river and Bibury)

Dinner: 7.15–8.30
Lunch: 12.15–1.45
Breakfast: 8.15–9.30

Children and dogs: Welcome

Open: Year-round

Special Features: Picturesque village; Centre of Cotswolds

Price: £

HOTEL: Buildings♡ Garden♡
AMENITIES: Fishing♡ Walks♥

The Swan Hotel is a typical English coaching inn originally at the ford across the River Colne at Bibury. Now the attractively creepered buildings look out over the picturesque gardens and 17th-century bridge in this delightful but touristy Cotswold village.

Colin Morgan, the proprietor, has been running the Swan for over seven years and has brought to it his own, obviously high, standards. The reception on our arrival was friendly and helpful and our room decorated in simple, fresh Sanderson wallpapers, had a wonderful view over the gardens and the neighbouring trout fishery. Each room has its own pleasant, but small, bathroom and my wife especially appreciated the built-in Braun hairdryer and the sweet scented Bronley soap. The double bed, although not expansive, was comfortable with cotton sheets.

Downstairs the Swan has a vivacious bar catering, in the main, for visitors, as opposed to residents, but a quiet 'lounge' area was also available. We in fact had a pleasant drink in the hotel gardens by the river admiring the views of this pretty village before sitting down to dinner in the large but gracefully designed dining room.

The food, like the menu, is simple but nonetheless of excellent standard in all departments. Colin Morgan takes great interest in obtaining the best possible ingredients. With meat and cheeses purchased from reliable sources in Cirencester, our beef was rare and delicious; my potted tongue was most unusual, but the pièce de résistance was my wife's chocolate mousse, subtlely laced with brandy. The Stilton was served in the most perfect condition.

Luckily, by dinner the majority of the considerable number of tourists in Bibury had dispersed and we were able to enjoy a pleasant post-prandial stroll through the village to enjoy the area's beauty, peace and calm.

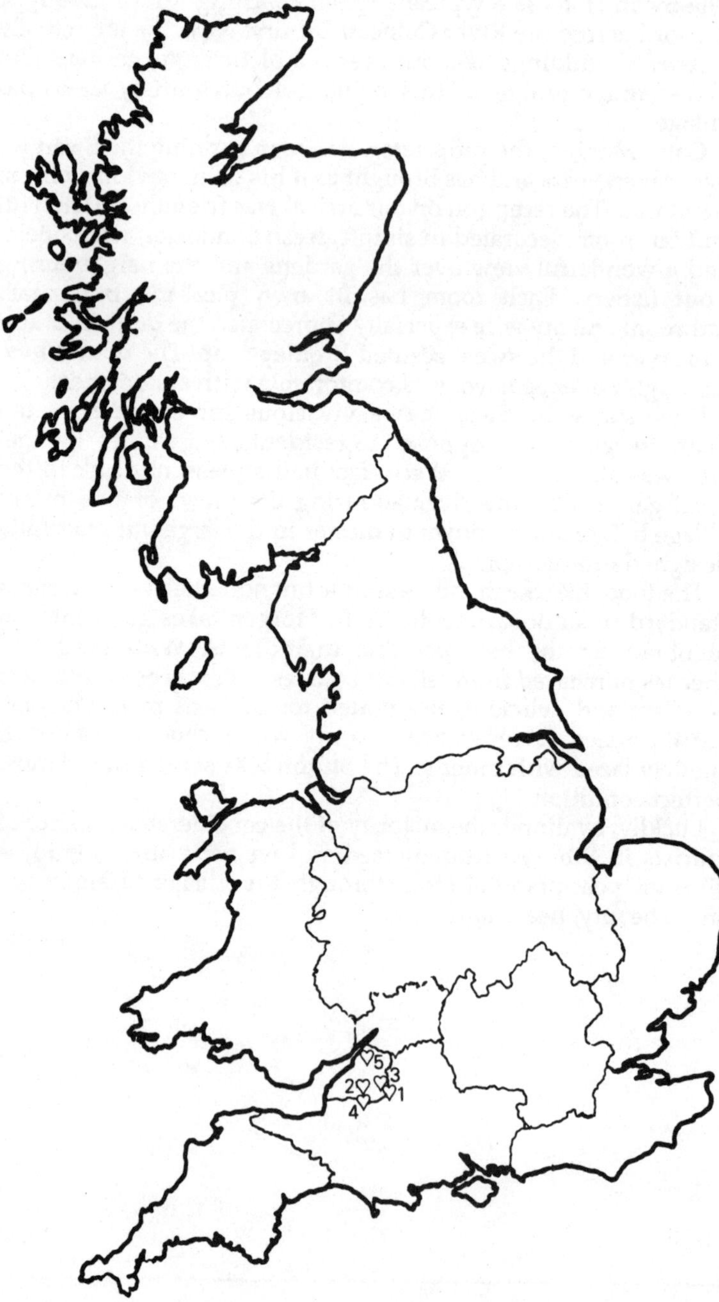
5
3
2
1
4

Avon

1 Homewood Park, Hinton Charterhouse, Avon
2 Hunstrete House, Chelwood, Avon
3 The Royal Crescent, Bath, Avon
4 Ston Easton Park, Farrington Gurney, Avon
5 Thornbury Castle, Thornbury, Avon

Homewood Park

Homewood Park
Hinton Charterhouse
Nr. Bath
Avon
BA3 6BB
Tel: Limpley Stoke (022122) 2643

Resident Owners: Stephen and Penny Ross

Cards: All

10 rooms (7 double beds)

Dinner: 7.00–9.30 7 nights a week
Lunch: 12.00–1.30
Breakfast: 7.30–9.30, English 8.00–9.30

Children: Tolerated but not encouraged
Dogs: No

Closed: 25 December – 14 January

Directions: 10 minutes drive from the centre of Bath on the A36 towards Warminster and Salisbury

Special Features: Drinks/meals outside; Close to Bath; American Museum; Pretty decor

Price: ££

HOTEL: Buildings♥ Rooms♥ Food♥ Wine♥ Garden/Grounds♡ Views♥
AMENITIES: Tennis♥ Riding♥ Croquet♥ Walks♥

Homewood Park is a small hotel and restaurant owned and run by Stephen and Penny Ross (previously of Popjoys in Bath). The house is a mixture of 18th-century and 19th-century set in flourishing gardens and woodlands with gentle views over the Limpley Stoke Valley.

Decor is traditional pastel shades, light and comfortable with original wood and lots of plants. The lounge has good individual pieces of furniture, an open fireplace and soft lighting. The dining room continues the soft pink and flowered look. The whole place has a gentle creative touch. Each dining table has a different small flower arrangement of wild flowers and grasses. All the rooms are individually decorated and have lovely views over lawns, woods and valley.

There is a big emphasis placed on the food, which we found excellent. Stephen Ross and Anthony Pitt produce a simple elegant meal that is refined and light. Very fresh ingredients make imaginative salads (most of the more exotic and expensive ingredients are home-grown). Vegetables were perfectly crisp and the whole meal is creatively presented, yet not fussy. There is usually a high proportion of fish dishes (on Thursdays a fixed priced fish menu), but always good local meat too. Desserts seem to provide plenty of scope for that creative style – only the hungry should take on the fromage blanc! A sensible wine list provides plenty of choice without pretention.

Homewood Park is really a restaurant with rooms and achieves an extremely high standard in a very pleasant informal atmosphere. We would have appreciated a real ice bucket – our only quibble.

There is a tennis court in the grounds and riding next door to work up an appetite for dinner.

The location is superb for exploring Bath and the many famous houses and gardens of the Avon area. The American Museum is just a few minutes away and is an absolute must. It contains a magnificent collection of reconstructed domestic scenes, furniture and patchwork.

Stephen and Penny and their small staff offer a very personal service. We found Homewood Park a delight and we are sure you will too.

Hunstrete House

Hunstrete House Hotel
Chelwood
Nr Bristol
Avon
BS18 4NS
Tel: 07618 578
Telex: 449540

Resident Proprietors: Thea and John Dupays

Cards: American Express, Visa

20 rooms (18 doubles, 2 four-posters; also 'Swallow Cottage' with private sitting room)

Dinner: 7.30–9.30 (9.00 on Sun)
Buffet Lunch: 12.45–2.00
Breakfast: Continental in room
7.30–10.00; English (in dining room only) 8–9.30

Children: No

Dogs: No

Open: Year-round (special winter rates November 1st–March 31st)

Directions: Take the A4 west out of Bath. Left on to the A39 to Marksbury. Hunstrete is on right between Marksbury and A37

Special Features: Beautiful house; Lovely garden and views

Price: ££

HOTEL: Buildings♥ Rooms♥ Food♥ Wine♥ Garden♥ Views♥
AMENITIES: Tennis♥ Swimming♥ Fishing♡ Riding♡ Croquet♡

Thea Dupays and her husband John are the fourth family to have owned Hunstrete House since monastic times, but surely the house has never looked so beautiful. Her taste is exquisite and she has achieved that almost impossible balance between the informality of a country house and the requirements of an efficient hotel.

The entrance hall, stairs and corridors are covered with a beautiful pink and buff floral wallpaper which sets the tone of the whole house. Mrs Dupays' own pictures are on the walls along with some by her ancestor who was an academician. The drawing room is beautiful without being pretentious, yet intimately arranged so that several groups can have their privacy.

The Dupays are great collectors; each piece of furniture is an excellent example and you must also look out for the special collections of embroideries, doorstops and Staffordshire figures. The House is always stuffed with lovely flowers; when we visited there were pots of fuchsias and geraniums, all from the unusual garden (the preserve of Mr Dupays) which combines flowerbeds with a vegetable garden. All is immaculately maintained by the three full-time gardeners.

Each room is named after a bird. We slept in 'Dove', furnished with a wonderful 18th-century painted and carved four-poster with green and pink silk hangings, ideally suited to watch TV, hidden in what looks like a chest of drawers, or see the deer grazing outside.

The restaurant is charming with the professional discreet service which exists throughout. Our dinner was of the same standard and quality of the hotel. I had 'Panache of Fish with Lobster Sauce and Cream' complemented by a good chablis, served in a silver wine coaster. We were pleased to be offered an excellent Cheddar (the Gorge is nearby) and Stilton along with good French cheeses.

The Dupays' Hunstrete has exquisite elegance and style combined with continuous attention to detail. It is a lovely place.

The Royal Crescent Hotel

The Royal Crescent Hotel
15/16 Royal Crescent
Bath
Avon
BA1 2LS
Tel: Bath (0225) 319090

Manager: Malcolm Walker

Cards: All

41 rooms (32 doubles, 1 four-poster, 2 suites and 'The Pavillion' – 2 doubles and 2 suites)

Dinner: 7.00–9.45
Lunch: 12.30–1.45
Breakfast: 7.30–10.00

Children: Welcome

Dogs: No
Open: Year-round
Special Features: Beautiful interiors; Centre of Bath
Price: £££

HOTEL: Buildings♥ Rooms♥ Food♥ Wine♥ Views♥

Two hundred years ago le tout Londres would regularly journey West to take the waters of Bath.

The Season was a glittering time for style and elegance, and the most prestigious address was the Royal Crescent with its magnificent sweeping views.

Now, thanks to a fine eye for detail and a seemingly unlimited bank balance, part of the Crescent has been lovingly restored and incorporated into an hotel that in 1981 prompted Egon Ronay to justly confer upon it his coveted Hotel of the Year Award.

Breathtakingly designed by Julie Hodge and jam-packed with fine antiques and period furniture, the hotel has a real country house flavour. Romantic weekenders can choose from 35 exquisite double bedrooms, including two spectacular suites in the newly opened Pavillion set back from the hotel which feature their own plant-filled conservatories complete with double whirl pools suitably filled with genuine spa water, brought from the Roman Baths below.

Dinner is a leisurely affair taken in the intimate candlelit restaurant, perhaps after a drink in the flower-filled bar or summer terrace. Chef Raymond Duthie has created a selection of scrumptious dishes in the nouvelle fashion. Try pureé of duck livers with foie gras and truffles followed by medallions of veal with cream cheese and sage. The wine list is extensive and contains a number of fine and favourite châteaux, not to mention some quite outstanding ports and brandies. Pink champagne can be discreetly delivered to the bedroom and is best enjoyed luxuriating in a deep bubblebath thoughtfully provided with soaps, shampoo, talc and soft towelling bathrobes.

Glance from the window and you will see the lights of Bath sparkling in the distance. Look hard along the cobbled street and you might even see the ghost of Beau Nash. He will be smiling with approval.

Ston Easton Park

Ston Easton Park
Ston Easton
Bath
Somerset
BA3 4DF
Tel: Chewton Mendip (076121) 631
Telex: 444738

Resident Proprietors: Peter and Christine Smedley

Cards: Diners, AMX, Access, Visa

16 rooms (14 doubles and twins, 5 four-posters)

Dinner: 7.30–9.30 (Sat till 10.00)
Lunch: 12.30–2.00
Breakfast: dining room 8.00–9.30, rooms 8.00–10.00 (Continental only in rooms)

Closed: January

Children: No

Dogs: Kennels in house

Directions: About 13 miles south of Bristol on the A37 between Farrington Gurney and Shepton Mallet.

Special Features: Palladian mansion; Grounds by Repton; Period decor

Price: £££

HOTEL: Buildings♥ Rooms♥ Food♥ Wine♥ Garden♥ Views♥
AMENITIES: Fishing♡ Croquet♥

If your idea of a romantic weekend is to stay in a beautifully decorated stately home, then Ston Easton Park is the place for you. The 18th-century house with its elegant Palladian style rooms immediately impresses. The saloon, glimpsed from the hall, is a magnificent, well-proportioned room with a superb plaster ceiling and carved pediments. It is furnished with the Smedleys' own antique furniture. In the centre stands a round table with a lovely flower arrangement, books and magazines, to be leafed through together on the comfortable sofas. When you sit down a maid will soon ask you what you wish to drink. For a more intimate atmosphere you can always sit in front of the fire in the library surrounded by the books in their mahogany bookcases. In the evening you should stroll down the little valley below the back of the house. A path leads you over a bridge and beside the tinkling river beneath the towering trees, planted after designs by Humphry Repton (the red book is in the house).

Each room is furnished with the same immaculate taste and is fresh, airy and charming. The principal bedrooms have four-poster beds. In ours the hangings matched the curtains and the bath was set in an alcove lined with marble, with little shell-shaped soaps. On the period dressing table an oval mirror reflected a beautiful fresh vase of flowers and a little petit-point pin cushion made by Christine Smedley.

We dined on quenelles of pike, calves' liver with julienne of leeks and ginger sour sauce matched with an excellent bottle of Meursault and a good Beaune finished off with the staggering tulip Ston Easton Park.

The Smedleys have made Ston Easton reflect their energy and enthusiasm; indeed their crest bears the hoteliers key in the beak of an eagle, yet the house retains its private country-house atmosphere. The place bursts with flower arrangements and lovely soft coloured azaleas in pots. The old servants' hall and wine cellar are still in use and there is a billiard room for rainy days and croquet on the lawn. You could not fail to leave Ston Easton without being bowled over – we were.

Thornbury Castle

Thornbury Castle
Thornbury
Bristol
BS12 1HH
Tel: Thornbury (0454) 412647
Telex: 449986 Castle G

Resident Owner: Kenneth Bell

Cards: All

10 rooms (4 doubles, 4 twins)

Dinner: 7.00–9.30
Lunch: 12.30–2.00
Breakfast: Continental in room from 7.30
English in dining room 8.00–9.30

Children: No

Dogs: No

Closed: 24th December – 30th December

Directions: Leave the M5 at exit 16. Take the A38 north to Alveston and then the B4061 to Thornbury.

Special Features: 16th-century castle; Vineyard; Helicopter landing

Price: £££

HOTEL: Buildings♥ Rooms♥ Food♥ Wine♥ Garden/Grounds♥ Views♡
AMENITIES: Fishing♡ Golf♡ Riding♡ Croquet♥ Walks♡

You can't get much more romantic than a castle set in its own walled gardens.

The entrance is through the vineyard planted with Muller Thurgau, producing about 1000 bottles a year. Or you can land your helicopter on the front lawn – but not if a good croquet game is in progress!

Thornbury was started in 1510 by the third Duke of Buckingham who hardly had time to finish it before Henry VIII had him on a one-way visit to Tower Hill and confiscated the lot. Henry had a romantic weekend or two there with Ann Boleyn and later Mary Tudor lived there.

The buildings and grounds are superb. A wonderful lovers' seat under the topiary is awaiting your visit.

Dining rooms (two) and lounges are panelled wood with huge fireplaces and lots of baronial bits and pieces. Some aspects of the decor need sorting out and simplifying, but then it's not easy to find furniture and fabric of castle proportions.

There are ten rooms, each individually decorated to a high standard and varying greatly in shape and configuration – our cosy little bathroom was down some steps from the bedroom and the main room door quite suitable for Alice in her shrinking stage. All charming stuff. The room in the octagonal tower is really special but lots of the others have beautiful oriel windows overlooking the gardens. Plumbing can't be easy in a stone castle but it worked well, as did the central heating. There are lots of nice little extras in the rooms to make life more comfortable.

Thornbury has a big reputation for its cuisine and is invariably praised by knowledgeable hoteliers and guests. It has been Egon Ronay Restaurant of the Year. Our lamb noisettes was mouth-watering and our various wines (Californian, selected by Kenneth Bell) were excellent. But we have had salmon better cooked, the vegetables could have been lighter and crisper and the Stilton was a bit disappointing. On the whole the food is traditional – eminently suitable for the environment – and Mr Bell certainly takes it and his wine seriously.

You will undoubtedly have a wonderful time – even if you don't have a helicopter.

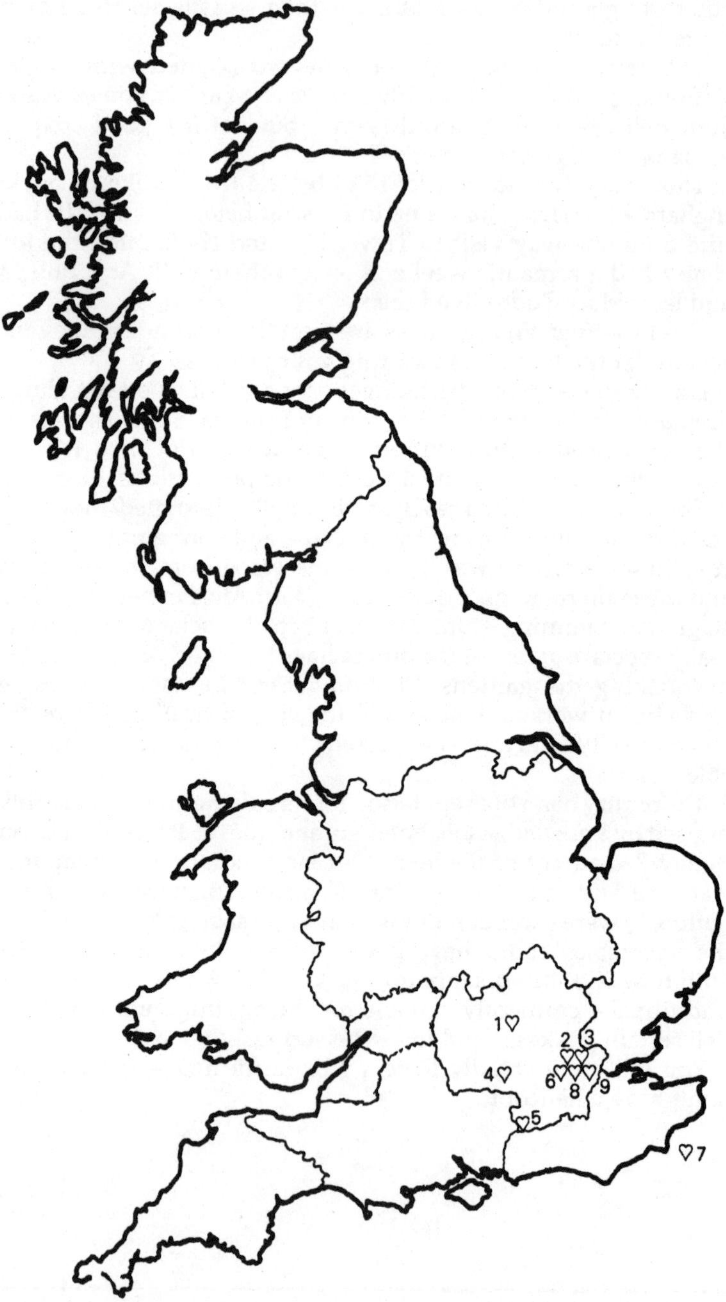
1
2
3
4
6
8
9
5
7

London & Home Counties

1. The Bell Inn, Aston Clinton, Buckinghamshire
2. Blakes, London, SW7
3. 11 Cadogan Gardens, London, SW3
4. The French Horn, Sonning, Berkshire
5. Lythe Hill Hotel, nr. Haslemere, Surrey
6. Number Sixteen Hotel, London, SW7
7. The Orient Express, London-Venice
8. The Ritz, London, W1
9. The Stafford, London, SW1

The Bell Inn

The Bell Inn
Aston Clinton
Bucks
HP22 5HP
Tel: Aylesbury (0296) 630252
Telex: 826715

Owner: Michael Harris

Cards: Access, Visa

21 rooms (all double or twin, all with private baths)

Dinner: 7.30–9.45
Lunch: 12.30–1.45
Breakfast: from 7.00

Children and dogs: Allowed if civilized

Open: Year round

Directions: On A41 four miles east of Aylesbury

Special Features: Outstanding food and wine; Lovely gardens; Good centre for visiting historic houses

Price: £££/££££

HOTEL: Buildings♥ Rooms♥ Food♥ Wine♥ Garden♥
AMENITIES: Croquet♥ Walks♡

The large bell inscribed by Paul Bocuse and the framed wine labels on the walls of the wood-panelled bar proclaim that Michael Harris's famous Inn is a temple of gastronomy. Over drinks Ugo, the courteous headwaiter who has been at The Bell for 22 years, will help you choose your meal and guide you through the spectacular wine list which offers a choice of some 400 wines, many of them rarities. The wines are remarkably good value; the food is expensive but the prices are justifiable: only fresh ingredients are used and many items, such as oysters and game are flown in directly from their source. Try the gravlax (which takes a week to prepare), local duckling, or fish en croute and, if you have room, finish with 'Bell Food' – an ambrosial dessert. The superb food is served on fine china, the wines in cutglass goblets; a silver candlestick gleams next to the decanter into which wine is poured in front of a flame to detect any sediment.

Fine restaurants do not necessarily make good hotels, but The Bell's standards are universally high. Five rooms are in the original 17th-century inn. Room No. 50 is particularly delightful, with painted furniture (including a four-poster) that's almost as old as the building. The other rooms, many of them suites, are across the road in a flower-filled stable yard behind which are extensive gardens and a croquet lawn. Most sumptuous is Apartment No. 16 with 'his-and-hers' baths, an antique mirrored bedhead, a log fire and its own garden. All rooms are attractively furnished and decorated, equipped with refrigerators filled with drinks. Hairdryers, bathrobes and good quality soaps make bathtime pleasant and there are many other thoughtful touches, including an umbrella.

Next morning, breakfast will appear, the table laid with delicate pink linen; fresh juices, good coffee, homemade breads (including pain au chocolat), excellent jam and any cooked dishes you like. A charming touch is the single rose, which you may keep.

Although Aylesbury's tentacles stretch uninvitingly towards Aston Clinton, there are many fine country houses to visit nearby. However, it is tempting to wander round the Inn's garden, laze on the patio or in the pretty sitting-room of one's suite and gather strength for the next outstanding meal.

Blakes

Blakes
33 Roland Gardens
London
SW7 3PE
Tel: 01-370 6701
Telex: 8813500

Owner: Anouska Hempel Weinberg

Manager: Leonard Burrows

Cards: All

70 rooms (60 doubles including some apartments)

Dinner: 7.30–11.30
Lunch: 12.30–2.30
Breakfast: 7.30–10.30, but can be served at any time

Children: If quiet

Dogs: No

Open: Year-round

Directions: Off Old Brompton Road. Note parking restrictions.

Special Features: Sauna; Outstanding decor; Central yet quiet location

Price: ££££

HOTEL: Buildings♡ Rooms♥ Food♥ Wine♥

Blakes is more than romantic – it is sensuous. Immense care has been devoted to the design of every detail. The glamorous owner, Anouska Hempel Weinberg, travels the world in search of more and more beautiful antique furniture and artefacts to delight the eye, though comfort isn't sacrificed for beauty. Sprawl on cushions, sipping drinks in the sumptuous Japanese alcove while considering the short but eclectic menu with the help of Patrice, the friendly and enthusiastic restaurant manager. The wine list, too, is short but extremely well-chosen; all the bottles are good quality, even at the cheaper end of the scale. The decor is as luxurious as the food: black and white, very elegant, with masses of bright flowers on each table and Oriental exotica on the walls. This is a place to see and be seen while enjoying one's delicious dinner. Everyone looks like a star and is treated like one; the famous can relax here with the infamous and the unknown.

And so to bed in your luxurious room or apartment, decorated in subtle colours to cocoon you in stylish comfort. No detail is ignored: beautiful furniture and objects everywhere, brass bedsteads heaped with cushions and pillowed with lace, luxury piled on luxury with inspired elegance. Mirrors in antique frames give a sense of space and light. Each room could feature (and probably has) in a glossy magazine and is frequently redecorated since materials are chosen for their effect rather than durability. Bathrooms, too, are lovely, provided with robes, large towels and Roger & Gallet soap. There are music centres, TVs and refrigerators in all apartments, food can be brought from the restaurant at dinner-time and room service is always available.

Under the care of Leonard Burrows, who runs the hotel with a discreet combination of efficiency and informality, Blakes is becoming even more beautiful as it grows, taking care never to lose that sense of intimacy. The price of all this does not come cheaply but this outstandingly innovative hotel is an experience not to be missed.

11 Cadogan Gardens

11 Cadogan Gardens
Sloane Square
London
SW3
Tel: 01-730 3426
Telex: 881 3318

Manager: Charles Harbord

Cards: None

60 rooms (20 doubles, 20 twins, including 4 suites. All have baths en suite. One four-poster)

Breakfast: 7.00–10.00. The hotel has no restaurant but comprehensive room service is provided and many restaurants are nearby (list of recommended restaurants available); also private dining room seating up to 12

Children: Allowed

Dogs: Not allowed

Open: Year-round

Directions: Parallel to Sloane Street, Sloane Square. Do not confuse with Cadogan Square or with Cadogan Hotel. Note parking restrictions.

Special Features: Conservatory; Very quiet yet central

Price: ££ (but remember this doesn't include dinner)

HOTEL: Buildings♡ Rooms♥ Garden♡
AMENITIES: Riding♡

Number 11 Cadogan Gardens is a haven for people of discerning taste, a country-house within minutes of Sloane Square. It is impossible to guess from the outside that this is an hotel. Ring the front door bell, step into the panelled hall and sign the visitors' book (there is no formal registration). Sinking back into your Victorian wing chair in the drawing room you can sip tea, eat scones with jam and clotted cream and admire the plants in the adjoining conservatory. There is a feeling of rural tranquillity. Guests have access to the private garden across the road, and riding in Hyde Park can be arranged to enhance the sense of country life in town.

The rooms are comfortably arranged using Victorian furniture in keeping with the style of the house. Throughout, elegance and tradition are thoughtfully combined with up-to-date efficiency and comfort. Each of the attractively decorated rooms has its own bathroom and there are many extra touches such as bowls of potpourri scenting the air. Some rooms have an adjoining private sitting room, comfortably furnished, tempting one to move in permanently.

The essence of Number 11 is to make guests feel at home; in fact, it is even better than being at home because the hall porters magically grant all one's wishes, including a chauffeur-driven Rolls-Royce Silver Shadow (at remarkably reasonable rates). There is no alcohol licence but the porters will gladly send out for a bottle; nor is there a restaurant but a delicious breakfast is served in the room with the morning papers.

When you leave Number 11 Cadogan Gardens (lady guests are given a box of potpourri on departure, as a reminder of the sweet-smelling atmosphere) you will feel a twinge of regret at having to face urban life again; but the friendly people who run this hotel so smoothly and discreetly will greet you like an old friend when you return, as you doubtless will.

The French Horn Hotel

The French Horn Hotel
Sonning-on-Thames
Berks
RG4 0TN
Tel: Reading (0734) 692204

Owners: Mrs Emmanuel and Mr J. F. F. Burns

Cards: Amex, Diners & Visa

5 rooms (2 doubles, 3 twins – 4 overlook the Thames – best suites Nos. 8 and 21)

Dinner: 7.15–9.30
Lunch: 12.15–2.00
Breakfast: 7.30–9.30 (English available in rooms)

Children: Welcome

Dogs: No

Open: Year-round

Directions: From Reading take the A4 towards Maidenhead turn left into Sonning through the village, turn left at T-junction, over the River, the Hotel is on the right

Special Features: Overlooking the Thames; Beautiful spot; Bedroom suites with the view

Price: ££

HOTEL: Buildings♡ Rooms♡ Food♡ Wine♡ Garden♡ Views♥
AMENITIES: Swimming♡ Fishing♡ Golf♡ Riding♡ Walks♥

The French Horn has the perfect site on a little backwater immediately overlooking the river Thames. The terrace, covered in creeper, provides a shady place to relax and look out over the lawns down to the River. We soon found ourselves sitting and idling away the evening over a bottle of Moselle watching the ducks and moor hens paddle past and the weeping willows sway gently in the breeze.

At last we tore ourselves away and went up to change in our room, No. 8, a nice little suite with its own balcony and the same lovely tranquil view of the river. The bed with its silver painted bedhead welcomed us with the sheets neatly turned down. The pink sofas gave us somewhere to sit down in private and enjoy our own company. After a long soak in the big and comfortable soft pink bath we went down to dinner.

We were shown a table beside the window where by now the flood lights had transformed the scene outside. The candles in their silver candelabra and soft lighting caught our mood as we enjoyed our dinner served with deft skill by the friendly and efficient waiters. Our white wine was served in silver goblets and the melba toast was so good we nearly forgot to leave room for a good homemade duck pâté and the speciality that week of sweetbreads. When the sweet trolley came round my wife insisted on the profiteroles almost drowned in cream. We took our coffee and a brandy on the terrace looking at the lights flicker on the surface of the water.

Next morning we started the day breakfasting on the balcony served in great style – everything seemed to be silver. We walked across the River into the pretty village of Sonning and explored the River with the occasional boat gently puttering by. On our way back we passed the Mill Theatre. If you stay a couple of nights at the French Horn you should go to a performance there, but not on a Saturday or Sunday night.

Mrs Emmanuel, who lives next door, continues to run this place with friendly efficiency. It is the perfect spot for honeymoon couples.

Lythe Hill Hotel

Lythe Hill Hotel
Petworth Road
Haslemere
Surrey GU27 3BQ
Tel: Haslemere (0428) 51251
Telex: 858402

General manager: Philip Ford

Cards: American Express, Visa, Diners Club, Access

6 rooms (In L'Auberge de France, all double with private bath; 1 four-poster)

Dinner: 7.15–10.45 (not Mon)
Lunch: 12.30–2.30
Breakfast: 8.15–9.30

(this information applies to L'Auberge de France)

Children: Allowed

Dogs: Allowed except in public rooms

Open: Year round

Directions: Nr (*not* in) Haslemere on B2131 between A286 and A283

Special Features: Lake in grounds (bring your own fishing rod); Sauna; Clay pigeon-shooting; Bowls; Many places of interest nearby

Price: ££

HOTEL: Buildings♥ Rooms♡ Food♥ Wine♥ Garden♥ Views♥
AMENITIES: Tennis♥ Fishing♥ Golf♡ Riding♡ Croquet♥ Walks♥

Nestled on a Surrey hillside, Lythe Hill is two hotels in one: L'Auberge de France and L'Entente Cordiale. We can believe that the latter has its fans, being light, clean and comfortable, but it is not the stuff of which this book is made. The 14th-century Auberge de France, however, has much to recommend it, particularly its fine restaurant where you can enjoy both classic French and nouvelle cuisine. Do ask, though, to be seated in the oak-panelled dining room with its inglenook – so much more romantic than the newly-modernized extension – and be sure to reserve a table when booking your room as this is a deservedly popular restaurant. Try the fish salad with saffron sauce, the entrecôte with roquefort in cider sauce (if you're feeling adventurous) and the kiwi-fruit mousse with strawberry coulis. The extensive wine list includes 25 clarets and service is attentive without being obtrusive. Altogether, a real gastronomic treat. Remember that food is the music of love . . .

L'Auberge de France has only six rooms, all different and decorated in period style with antique furniture for the most part. Beams and some uneven floors add authenticity (beware if you're tall) and the 14th-century half-timbered building has, on the whole, been well adapted for 20th-century living.

L'Auberge is due for redecoration and one hopes that its considerable charm will be maintained and even enhanced by the sympathetic use of colours and fabrics. It is certainly worth a visit for the food and an enjoyable experience to stay in such an ancient house. Lythe Hill is an excellent centre for visiting historic houses, pretty Sussex villages, and for walking in the miles of adjacent National Trust woodland.

Number Sixteen

Number Sixteen
16 Sumner Place
London
SW7 3EG
Tel: 01-589 5232
Telex: 266638 WATSON

Owner: Michael Watson

Cards: All

25 rooms (20 doubles, all with showers; 'best doubles' have baths as well)

Breakfast: till 11.30
Lunch and dinner not provided but many restaurants nearby (a list of recommended restaurants is placed in all bedrooms)

Children: Allowed but not encouraged under 12

Dogs: No

Open: Year-round

Direction: Off Old Brompton Road nr South Kensington. Note parking restrictions but taxis and public transport easily available

Special Features: Attractive garden; Atmosphere of private house

Price: £ (doesn't include dinner)

HOTEL: Buildings♡ Rooms♥ Garden♥

The owner of this congenial hotel tends his guests as carefully as his flower-filled garden, a tranquil oasis where one can relax only a few yards from the hurly-burly of South Kensington. Indeed, the whole hotel is an oasis to which contented guests, who enjoy the care taken of them and the combined elegance and warmth of the ambiance, regularly return. Many have musical or theatrical connections and a high proportion of them are American. A number of leading country hoteliers use Number Sixteen as their London base – a real accolade.

The atmosphere is that of a private house: guests are given a key to the front door and help themselves to drinks in the comfortable sitting room. Throughout the building (which consists of three inter-linked Victorian houses) bright but tasteful colours, antique furniture and an eclectic choice of paintings emphasize the sense of staying in an elegant town residence rather than an hotel.

You will *not* find at Number Sixteen butter wrapped in foil and nasty little plastic pots of jam; nor wire coathangers, for that matter. The refrigerator in each room is stocked with mixers for drinks and further provisions can be bought from nearby shops, dispensing with the need for room service. At least one of the highly trained assistants is, however, constantly on call and there are many excellent restaurants within walking distance.

Not surprisingly, the hotel is almost always full and as much advance warning as possible is therefore recommended. The proportion of staff to guests is high; service is friendly and discreet with attention to detail sadly lacking in many larger hotels. The rooms facing the garden, two of which have private patios, are especially recommended. Throughout this 'home from home' you will find comfort, style and bonhomie.

The Orient Express

Orient Express (Venice Simplon Orient Express)
Victoria Station, London–Venice
Reservations:
Sea Containers House
20 Upper Ground
London
SE1 9PD
Tel: London (01) 928 5837
Telex: 8955803

Cards: All

Travel time: 24-hours. Leaves Victoria Station Fri 11.44

Train carries: About 300 people

Dinner: 8.00 and 10.30 (black tie recommended)

Open: 16 March–11 Nov.
Special Features: Unique experience; Truly romantic
Price: ££££

HOTEL: Rooms♥ Food♥ Wine♥ Views♥

The Orient Express spells Romance. Skip work on Friday, set your clock back to the Age of the Train and arrive in the city of eternal beauty and romance: Venice. Nip back on the plane on Sunday night.

The experience starts at a special platform at Victoria Station where the young, smart and enthusiastic staff check you in and whisk your luggage on to the train – hold on to your passport and camera as your luggage next appears in your cabin at Boulogne. Tuck into a very good cold lunch accompanied by quantities of champagne in the restored Pullmans, plush with their armchairs, thick damask tablecloths and Lalique glass all made specially for the train.

The low spot of the journey is the Channel crossing in a reserved section of a Sealink ferry – sleep off your lunch. A few steps in Boulogne and your sleeping car attendant welcomes you aboard and shows you to your cabin – a mirrored marqueterie box with its own corner basin and padded ladder to the top bunk. Then it's time to dress for dinner, a wonderful four-course affair – we started with real foie gras. Have a bottle of chablis: you pass the vineyards en route. Having finished dinner take your coffee in the bar car, listen to the tinkling of the ivories from the baby grand, gather up a brandy and take the air on the platform in Paris.

A discreet knock on the door next morning brings steaming coffee with fresh croissants and spectacular views of the Alps. Make your way to the bar to enjoy the exceptional changing panorama of Lake Maggiore. Meanwhile, in your cabin the bunks and sheets have vanished and there you have your own private compartment to enjoy the flat plains of Italy before arriving in Venice. You can either take brunch on the train but the canny romantics can guzzle a picnic in private bought at Milan Station.

You arrive in Venice to drop into a launch which sweeps you down the Grand Canal (steal a kiss under the Rialto Bridge). Stay at the Cipriani, the Danieli or book room 452 at the Europa and Regina – it has an enormous balcony overlooking the Grand Canal. This is the view which is the sequel to the memorable train journey.

The Ritz

The Ritz
Piccadilly
London
W1V 9DG
Tel: London (01) 493 8181
Telex: 267200

General Manager: Michael Duffell

Cards: All

139 rooms (29 doubles, 46 twins; 9 one-bed suites, 6 two-bed suites)

Dinner: 6.30–11.00 (10.00 on Sun)
Lunch: 12.00–2.00
Breakfast: 7.30–10.00

24-hour full room service

Children: Welcome

Dogs: No, but can be accommodated

Open: Year-round

Special Features: Luxurious decor; Imaginative new chef

Price: ££££ Special weekend rates

HOTEL: Buildings♥ Rooms♥ Food♥ Wine♥ Garden♡ Views♡

The Ritz remains the epitome of the romantic hotel born an instant smash hit at the height of the Edwardian Era. At a time of extreme wealth no expense was spared: marbles were imported from the four corners of the globe and the interior was decorated in the fashionable Louis XVI style. Such was the workmanship little has needed to be changed since its opening in 1906. However, in the last few years new life has been injected into the old vessel. Michael Duffell has taken over the management and Michael Quinn has become the chef.

The rooms retain their brass coal scuttles by the fireplaces, and the brass umbrella stands beside the door. Many rooms still have the original brass beds. The old bathrooms have, alas, gone and are replaced by opulent modern ones which all include a shower as well as the bath and two bath mats. The sandalwood soap is the Ritz's own and is monogrammed to match the huge towels and the linen. The pillows are especially large to rest not only your head but also your shoulder, meanwhile the general decor of the rooms with its plaster swags and mouldings is of a soft pastel, here creating a haven of luxurious calm from the traffic and bustle outside.

The Ritz is still famous for its teas in the Palm Court, the little orchestra plays on, evoking memories of past liaisons. If you dream too long you will find yourself drinking an exotic dusty-pink Ritz champagne cocktail or sampling some of their own champagne. But it is in the restaurant that you discover the new energy and enthusiasm of Michael Quinn who talks about food as others might about ballet: 'Cooking is giving with truth and sincerity, taking the humblest ingredient and handling it with love.' He has created a new team who share his ideals, replaced the china and rewritten the menu in English. He believes passionately that the English can cook just as well as the French. We had a wonderful meal to prove it including a clever fish terrine, crystals of iced champagne and a filet of lamb with pulses. The choice of wines is, of course, extensive.

The Stafford Hotel

The Stafford Hotel
St James's Place
London SW1A 1NJ
Tel: London (01) 493 0111
Telex: 28602

Managing Director: Terry Holmes

Cards: Amex

65 rooms (5 suites, 57 doubles)

Dinner: 6.30–10.30
Lunch: 12.30–2.45
Breakfast: 7.00–11.00 (from 7.30 downstairs)
24-hour room service, full menu until 10.30, then limited menu

Children: Welcome

Dogs: No

Open: Year-round

Directions: Just off St James's Street on left-hand side about half way up is St James's Place. The Hotel is at the end round the corner

Special Features: Calm haven; Friendly formality; Good bar

Price: ££££

HOTEL: Buildings♡ Rooms♥ Food♡ Wine♥ Garden♡

Only the discerning few realize that lurking behind the busy St James's with its view of St James's Palace is one of London's quietest and most refined hotels. Once you have checked in at the front door, you visit the Stafford through the mews off St James's, into the intimate little bar at the back of the Hotel. On hot summer evenings you can enjoy their perfect Pimms sitting al fresco in a garden chair painted with lilies of the valley. It is a peaceful little nook of greenery with scented walls of honeysuckle, and a couple of bay trees for shade, surrounded by the original mews houses with their baskets of flowers hung off the railings. The bustle of London is far away with only the sound of ice clinking in glasses and the subdued conversation of the other cogniscenti who delight in this haven.

You will find the staff efficient and relaxed with a pervading understated formality. Our bedroom had the same quiet elegance which is the hallmark of the Hotel, approached by a soft pink corridor, the buff textured wallpaper sets off the lovely little soft tinted original flower prints on the walls. Two cushions lay welcoming on the chintz bedspread. We watched the remote controlled TV firmly tucked up in bed and never moved again. The bathroom continued the pink theme with pink tiles of the floor matched with pretty tiles of flowers with the occasional Bo-Peep on the wall. The monogrammed bathrobes are truly luxurious as is the old-fashioned shower which cascades buckets of water.

The head waiter who presented us with our menus seemed keen to show his skill with a flambé dish so we chose the steak au poivre which was, indeed, finished off with theatrical style in a great woosh of flames by our table. Terry Holmes spoiled us dreadfully by taking us down to see his original 18th-century cellars stocked with superb wines and then gave us a bottle of Chateau Palmer '70 to drink with our dinner, which was, of course, quite exquisite. The Hotel boasts two master someliers who will ably guide you to similar delights.

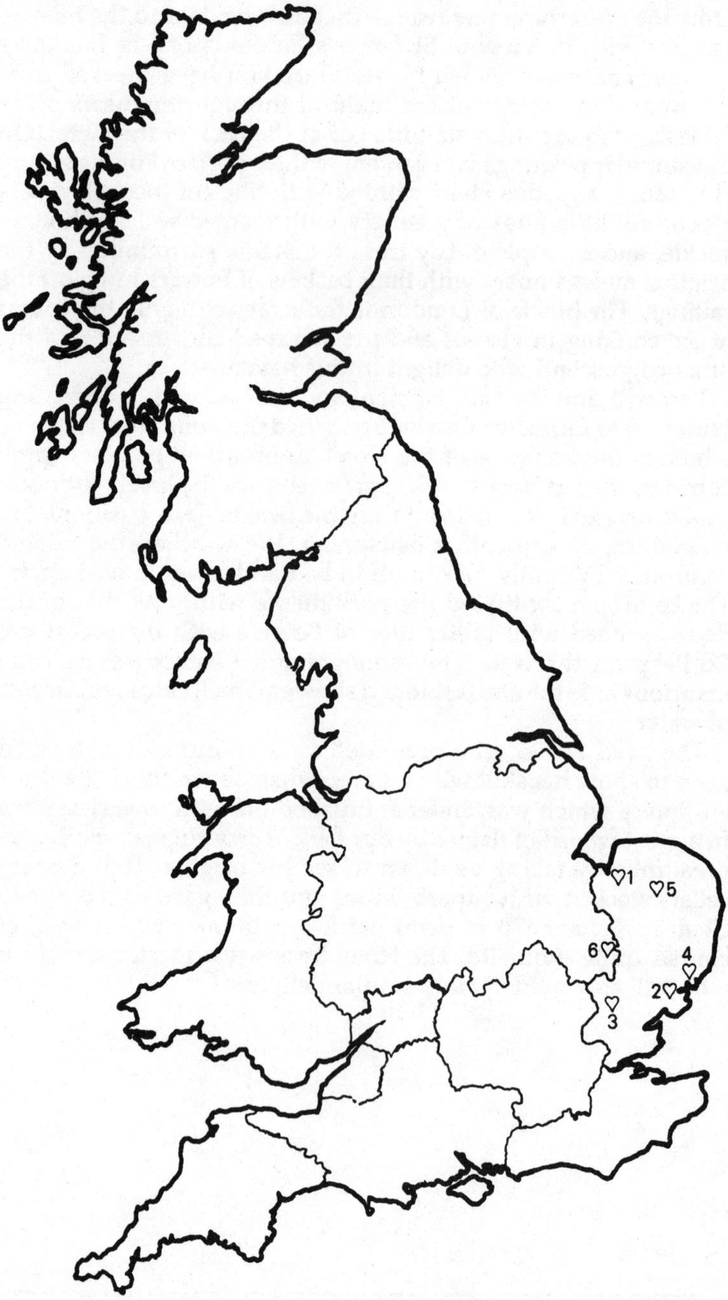
1
5
6
4
2
3

East Anglia

1. Congham Hall, Grimston, Norfolk
2. Maison Talbooth, Dedham, Essex
3. Priors Hall, Stebbing, Essex
4. Seckford Hall Hotel, Woodbridge, Suffolk
5. Shipdham Place, Shipdham, Norfolk
6. Swynford Paddocks, Newmarket, Suffolk

Congham Hall

Congham Hall
Kings Lynn
Norfolk
PE32 1AH
Tel: Hillington (0485) 600250

Resident Proprietors: The Forecast Family

Cards: AMX, Visa, Diners

9 rooms (1 four-poster, 7 doubles)

Dinner: 7.30–9.30
Lunch: 12.30–2.00
Breakfast: 7.30–9.30 (Sun from 8.30)
Light breakfast with an egg available in room

Children: None under 12

Dogs: No, but kenneling available outside

Open: 14 January–24 December

Directions: From Kings Lynn take A149 towards Cromer to 2nd roundabout, right on to A148 Sandringham/Fakenham road. 100 yards turn right to Grimston, drive straight for 2½ miles. Hotel is on left-hand side.

Special Features: Excellent food; Pretty grounds and walks; Jacuzzi

Price: £

HOTEL: Buildings♡ Rooms♡ Food♥ Wine♡ Garden♡ Views♡
AMENITIES: Tennis♥ Swimming♥ Fishing♡ Golf♡ Riding♡ Beach♡ Sailing♡ Croquet♥ Walks♥

Congham Hall is the new home of the charming and energetic Forecast family who have created a lovely hotel out of this large country house next door to Sandringham.

When we arrived, there was Mrs Forecast at the door to welcome us. They have a secret device warning them of your arrival. We were immediately made to feel at home and shown up the unusual curved staircase to our room which sported a lovely four-poster bed. In this bed you really draw all the curtains to make a truly romantic nook. As it was mid-afternoon we took an apple each from the bowl at the end of our bed and with two long cool ciders we popped through a hedge across the drive to find the cricket pitch where we lazed away several hours watching the game from the shade beneath a huge and ancient oak tree. When the game ended we wandered off across the fields to find the charming, pretty litte Congham Church with its long leafy avenue of limes still with the occasional piece of confetti on the path. On our way back we walked round the house's gardens to find the kitchen garden full of flowers ready for cutting, destined for the house, and rows of vegetables grown for John McGeever, the young chef, to weave his culinary magic.

Back in our room we scorned the large oval corner bath for a jacuzzi, but we did appreciate the plants in the bathroom the next day. Downstairs we found ourselves a magnificent sofa in a quiet corner of the drawing room where we were treated to smoked salmon and fresh crab canapes with our drinks as we discussed our choice for dinner and the time so as to fit in with the chef who works alone staggering the meals to give his whole attention to each. We were delighted with the friendly and efficient service producing an exquisite dinner. Everything relies totally on the season's offerings. We had a carré of lamb with lemon, lime and fresh sage and a knock-out strawberry sorbet.

Here is a small hotel destined for stardom. With their lovely setting and dedicated efforts this place cannot fail to become a haven for romantics. As it is still very new it is remarkable value, with the touches and cuisine of hotels twice its price.

Maison Talbooth

Maison Talbooth
Dedham
Colchester
Essex
CO7 6HN
Tel: (0206) 322367

Owner: Gerald Milsom

Cards: Access, Amex, Diners, Visa

10 rooms (8 doubles, 2 twins)

Dinner: 7.00–9.30
Lunch: 12.30–2.00
Breakfast: 7.00–9.30 (English from 7.30)

Children: Not encouraged (babysitting arranged)

Dogs: No

Open: Year-round

Directions: From Colchester take to A137 to Ardleigh turn left on the B1029 towards Dedham. Turn left towards Stratford St Mary, Maison Talbooth is on left-hand side.

Special Features: Le Talbooth Restaurant; River Stour

Price: £££

HOTEL: Buildings♥ Rooms♥ Food♥ Wine♥ Garden♡ Views♡
AMENITIES: Tennis♥ Walks♥

128

The Maison Talbooth proved to be a delightful experience in weekending. As we left the A12 we drove down a meandering country road that brought us to the front of the charming Victorian-style hotel, just one mile from the picturesque village of Dedham. The drive in itself was a delight and for those who enjoy a gentle stroll whilst admiring lush farmland, the ten-minute walk to Dedham is perfect.

The hotel staff are young, enthusiastic and very welcoming. Having arrived late in the afternoon, we were brought tea and biscuits in the drawing room, where an open fire already burned as we sank into a soft sumptuous couch.

The house is beautifully maintained, with a cool mustard exterior that complements the landscape, whilst the interior is decorated in soft pastels and cool shades of ivory. The spacious rooms are light, airy and tastefully furnished. Each room is named after a poet; ours was called 'Keats' and it came with an enormous bathroom that boasted a circular sunken bath ideal for two. We thought it was very romantic! We also had a private patio garden which, had the weather been better, would have provided an excellent setting for a pre-dinner drink by moonlight or a secluded breakfast.

A short walk from the hotel is Le Talbooth Restaurant. The fact that the restaurant is not attached to the hotel may prove inconvenient to some. However, we found it extremely pleasant wandering off to the restaurant for early evening drinks (the hotel, if you wish, will collect you at your leisure), and enjoyed the peace and quiet. The restaurant is located on the edge of the River Stour, it is a breathtaking 16th-century timber-framed house, with facilities for drinks on the terrace (weather permitting) or in the bar. The contrast in style between the hotel and the restaurant is refreshing, yet something that remains unchanged is the chatty, helpful nature of the staff. The food is spectacular as befits one of the privileged few restaurants in England with a Michelin star. The wine list is extremely comprehensive and made a lot simpler by the knowledgeable staff. It includes a large choice of champagnes, any of which can be served in the circular bubble bath by discreet waiters.

We found Maison Talbooth to be both interesting and charming, and would find it very difficult to fault. It is ideal for a stay, romantic or otherwise.

Prior's Hall

Prior's Hall
Parsonage Farm
Stebbing
Nr Great Dunmow
Essex
CM6 3SW
Tel: Stebbing (037186) 316 or 532
Telex: 4444337 ACTBUS G HERITAGE

Owners: Major and Mrs F. W. R. Fisher

Cards: All, though cheque preferred

5 rooms (all double with bath en suite)

Dinner: 8 (or later by prior arrangement)
Lunch: By arrangement (picnics available on request)
Breakfast: Any time till 12.00

Children: Over 14

Dogs: No (several in residence)

Closed: 23 December–31 January

Directions: Follow signs for Stebbing off A120 between Great Dunmow and Braintree. Unobtrusive entrance opposite church.

Special Features: Historic building; Good centre for exploring East Anglia; Part of The Heritage Circle of historic houses throughout Britain which welcome guests. For information about other houses, contact: John Denning, Burghope Manor, Winsley, nr Bradford-on-Avon, Wilts (Tel: 022 122 3557)

Price: ££

HOTEL: Buildings♥ Rooms♡ Food♡ Wine♡ Garden♡
AMENITIES: Swimming♥ Walks♡

Prior's Hall is part of The Heritage Circle whose members welcome guests into their comfortable and beautiful historic houses. Major and Mrs Bill Fisher are both colourful characters who have achieved a balance between the informality and cosiness of a private country house and the amenities one expects from an hotel, though the emphasis is definitely on the family atmosphere. Animal-lovers will adore Prior's Hall: dogs, cats and occasionally a tame goose wander through the fine half-timbered house. In the yard, 14 peacocks, more geese and a retired horse contribute to the engaging eccentricity of the household.

Most of the bedrooms are in the medieval part of the house, comfortably furnished with the Fishers's own antiques and ornaments enhancing the charming exposed timbers, brick fireplaces and leaded windows that look out on to pleasant gardens. Each has its own bathroom ingeniously tucked into the available space. As the Fishers stress, there are no rules at Prior's Hall – it's like staying with a benevolent aunt and uncle. You can breakfast as late as noon (by the indoor swimming pool, if you like) and there is no official check-out time.

After a day of country pursuits (the Major will lend you maps of the little-known but delightful locality), relax by a blazing log fire. If you are feeling sociable, join the Major and his other guests in the candlelit dining room with family portraits gazing down from the dark panelling, where generous portions – cooked with excellent ingredients under Mrs Fisher's watchful eye – are served. However, they will quite understand if you would prefer to dine à deux in one of the other lovely rooms, outside on the terrace, or even in the privacy of your bedroom. We were pleased with Major Fisher's recommendation of a local wine from nearby Suffolk – another example of the personal touch which makes Prior's Hall a special experience.

Seckford Hall

Seckford Hall Hotel
Woodbridge
Suffolk
IP13 6NU
Tel: Woodbridge (039 43) 5678

Resident Directors: Mr and Mrs M. S. Bunn

Cards: All

24 rooms (4 four-posters, 7 doubles, 8 twins)

Dinner: 7.30–9.30 (advise if arrival after 9.00)
Lunch: 12.30–2.00
Breakfast: 7.30–9.30, English downstairs

Children and dogs: Welcome

Open: Year-round

Directions: Take the A12 from Ipswich towards Woodbridge. Two miles before Woodbridge you will see the sign on the left-hand side.

Special Features: Elizabethan manor house; Beautiful gardens and lake

Price: £ (special rates available)

HOTEL: Buildings♥ Rooms♥ Garden♡
AMENITIES: Fishing♡

Set in beautifully kept grounds, Seckford Hall nestles in the countryside just inland from the sea at Woodbridge. The magnificent Tudor exterior is well-matched inside, the Hall having been lovingly restored after years of neglect and an army occupation during the last war.

Our room alone made the two-hour journey from London well worthwhile with a splendid, extremely comfortable, four-poster bed with Tudor-style furniture. A lot of trouble had been taken with the room including a pretty vase of flowers on our chest of drawers. Even the wastepaper baskets had a picture of Seckford Hall on them. In fact, all rooms had extremely charming finishing touches. Our bathroom was really rather small, but the colour scheme was pleasing and the water hot.

Arriving on the first warm evening of the summer, we were able to sit out on our magnificent balcony, covered with wistaria, before descending to dinner. The attentive staff showed us to our corner table and we were able to choose from a reasonably extensive menu. We had fresh lobster selected for us from the hotel's own lobster tank.

Michael Bunn, the proprietor, who lives with his family in the east wing of Seckford Hall, creates a most welcoming atmosphere amongst his 52 staff. He shows the English flag in his wine list so we enjoyed a refreshing and reasonably priced Suffolk white wine.

One of the charms of the hotel is the intimate proportion of the reception rooms where we had delicious coffee and chocolates after dinner. The pièce de résistance, though, is the main hall and its multicoloured figurative carpet featuring medieval kings and queens.

Breakfast could be had in our room, but we made our way to the dining room with our newspapers, where we started the day with kippers fresh from the Orford smokery, and good strong coffee.

As we left, we were delighted to see the signed photograph of Margaret Thatcher, who had recently visited the hotel.

Shipdham Place

Shipdham Place Hotel
Church Close
Shipdham
Nr Thetford
Norfolk
IP25 7LX
Tel: Dereham (0362) 820303

Proprietors: Melanie and Justin de Blank

Cards: None, must book in advance, deposit required

5 rooms (2 with double beds, all with private bathrooms, one not en suite)

Dinner: 7.30–8.30. Closed Tues except by special arrangement

Breakfast: 8.30–9.30 English in dining room only

Children: No

Dogs: No

Open: Mid-March to mid-December, Thursdays to Sundays in January, part February and March. Sometimes closed when de Blanks away

Special Features: Private home atmosphere. Superb food and wine

Price: ££

HOTEL: Rooms♡ Food♥ Wine♥

Shipdham Place, the home of Melanie and Justin de Blank, is a typical Norfolk old rectory just opposite the pretty church of Shipdham. The Hotel is at the sign of a sheep with black Welsh mountain sheep grazing on the lawn.

There are only five rooms, all of which are charming. They have been decorated by Melanie de Blank with Laura Ashley wallpaper with matching curtains, wicker chairs and attractive mahogany furniture. Our room had a lovely writing desk stuffed with books and on the chest of drawers was a pile of *Country Life* and *House & Garden* beside a plate of fresh fruit. There are lots of nice touches: a marble top for the oval basin with its Norfolk lavender soap on a Limoges saucer, wooden loo seats and a big brass bolt on the door to ensure privacy.

Justin de Blank is a real connoisseur of food and his knowledge of wine is particularly extensive. One of the main reasons for going to Shipdham is to eat there. You make your own drinks and meet in the drawing room where you discuss the wine which will go with the five-course fixed menu, changed each day. He particularly encourages one to drink a couple of half-bottles with your dinner to complement both the fish and the meat, the Sancerre was superb and the claret interesting. They perfectly complemented the superb dinner cooked by Melanie de Blank. We had poached fillet of brill with chive sauce, fillet of beef with mustard and tarragon sauce, salad, cheese and hot apple tartlets. The cheeses require particular mention as they are imported from France and are especially good, as are the liqueurs.

Whilst Continental breakfast can be served in the room, you have to eat the 'proper' breakfast in the dining room with real, freshly squeezed orange juice, pink grapefruit, special sausages and free-range eggs.

Staying at Shipdham Place is for those who really appreciate good food in a family house which just happens to be a hotel.

Swynford Paddocks

Swynford Paddocks
Six Mile Bottom
Newmarket
Suffolk
CB8 OUQ
Tel: Six Mile Bottom (063 870) 234

Resident Owner: Ian Bryant

Cards: AMEX, Access, Visa, Diners

12 rooms (4 doubles, 5 twins)

Dinner: 7.30–9.00 (Sun 7.30–8.30)
Lunch: 12.30–1.45
Breakfast: 7.30–9.30 (weekends 10.00)
English available in rooms

Children: Welcome

Dogs: (Small) welcome

Open: Year-round

Directions: Drive out of Newmarket towards London. Six Mile Bottom is on the old A11. The hotel is about 5 miles on the right hand side.

Special Features: Stud farm; Byronic scandal; Newmarket races

Price: ££

HOTEL: Food♡ Wine♡ Garden/Grounds♡ Views♡
AMENITIES: Tennis♥ Golf♡ Riding♡ Croquet♥ Mini-golf♥ Walks♡

You will be following in the footsteps of that mysteriously romantic poet Lord Byron when you arrive at Swynford Paddocks, in the heart of Newmarket stud farm country. But not following too closely we hope, because it was here that he had a scandalous romantic encounter with his half-sister Augusta that rocked society in 1813. The house, then known as The Lodge, belonged to her husband Colonel Leigh, and there was much gossip as to the paternity of young Medora, a daughter born to Augusta the following year.

The large and rambling building with a mixture of architectural styles has been added to by subsequent owners including Lord Derby (who named the place after his favourite racehorse, Swynford) and the De la Rue family of bank-note fame. It now belongs to Ian and Jane Bryant who aim to give it the atmosphere of a country house hotel.

In this the Bryants are quite successful – indeed the spacious bedrooms (all individually furnished) have the feel of your favourite aunt's spare bedroom with books and flowers by the bed. Each room has a TV and private bathroom, though you must specify if you want a double bed. In the morning we drew back the curtains to a view of misty fields and paddocks.

An impressively panelled entrance hall leads on to comfortable and tastefully decorated sitting rooms. The dining room is also panelled and modest in size, offering a high standard of cuisine with mainly English dishes. We ate from an excellent à la carte menu and our meal included chicken and spinach terrine, roast saddle of hare with fresh vegetables – all beautifully presented – accompanied by a bottle of Chateau Siran '76, an interesting claret which, according to Ian Bryant, came from the first antinuclear cellar in Bordeaux. The carefully chosen and well annotated wine list is certainly worthy of special attention.

Swynford Paddocks has pleasant gardens with a croquet lawn, tennis court and mini golf. There is also the stud farm next door to explore, but for those wishing to ride, the hotel will make arrangements at a nearby riding stables.

The hotel is relaxing and almost too peaceful but well located for racing buffs being just six miles from Newmarket, and close enough to Cambridge for a picnic on a punt. Best to leave your sister at home.

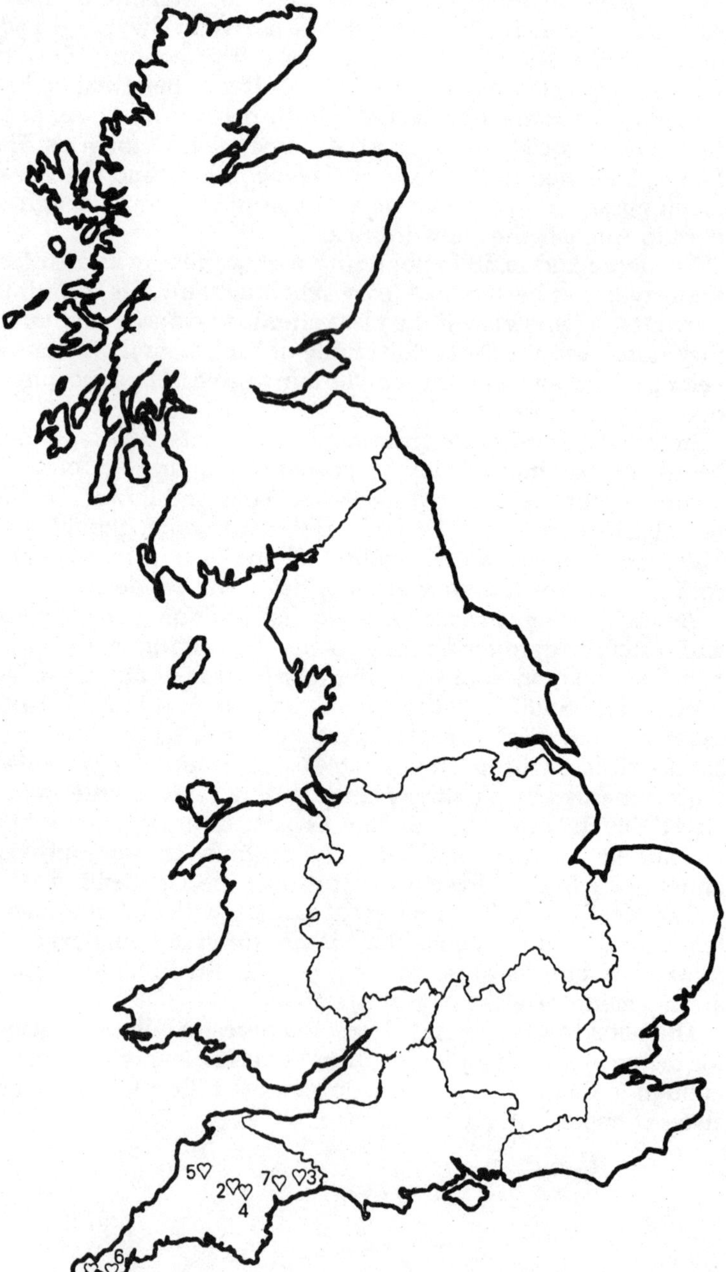
5
2
4
7
3
6
1

Devon & Cornwall

1 The Abbey Hotel, Penzance, Cornwall
2 Bly House, Chagford, Devon
3 Combe House, Gittisham, Devon
4 Gidleigh Park, Chagford, Devon
5 Half Moon Inn, Sheepwash, Devon
6 Riverside, Helford, Cornwall
7 Woodhayes, Whimple, Devon

The Abbey

The Abbey
Penzance
Cornwall
TR18 4AR
Tel: (0736) 66906

Resident Owners: Jean and Michael Cox

Cards: None

7 rooms (All doubles, 5 double beds; (rooms 1 and 3 are most romantic)

Dinner: At or around 8.00 (when it's cooked)
Lunch: Not normally
Breakfast: 8.00–9.30

Children: Over 10

Dogs: Only well-behaved

Closed: November to March

Directions: In Penzance above the harbour and below the abbey

Special Features: Very personal touch (antiques); Antique bathrooms; St Michael's Mount

Price: £

HOTEL: Buildings♡ Rooms♥ Food♡ Garden♡
AMENITIES: Tennis♡ Swimming♡ Fishing♡ Riding♡ Beach♡ Sailing♡ Walks♡

140

The Abbey is a charming little townhouse that hides on a steep hill overlooking Penzance harbour and St Michael's Mount beyond. It is not easy to find but unmistakably the place you are looking for once you see it – despite the fact that the little signboard is hidden behind the hedge.

Lots of powder blue, white and natural wood provide the setting for the entirely personal collection of antique furniture and decoration assembled by Jean and Michael Cox.

You can sink into comfortable chintzy sofas in the light, airy first floor drawing room overlooking the little garden and courtyard behind the house. There are plentiful plants and fresh flowers and lots of lovely little antique bits and pieces. This is a great place for romantic chat and mutual seduction – open a bottle of wine and enjoy the almost year round open fire.

The central staircase leads down to the dining room with individual antique tables and another permanent open fire. Dinner was simple and delicious – a super homemade thick vegetable soup and either local sole, scallops and mushrooms or a grilled pork chop. The apple crumble was great, and the cream . . .

Our bedroom was one of the most romantic we have had. With real old patchworks, comfortable armchairs and decorative curtained headboard bed. Little white painted church windows catch the sun in the morning and provide misty views out over the harbour.

The atmosphere is entirely that of a private house. You are given a front door key but there are no room keys. The owners are friendly but discreet. Michael has professional training in hotel and catering – but then he does in other things too. Jean was apparently in antiques but observant guests may wonder about this. How many antique collectors in Penzance have the latest copies of *Interview* lying about the drawing room.

The Abbey is a great place for fun in the bath. You can both sit in the superb antique bath sipping a drink with a view of the garden – but mind you don't knock over the potted plants or the china soap dish.

Bly House

Bly House
Nattadon Hill
Chagford
Devon
TQ13 8BW
Tel: Chagford (064 73) 2404

Resident owners: Mr and Mrs G. B. Thompson

Cards: None

8 rooms (5 with bathrooms, 1 double four-poster, 1 double half-tester, 3 twins)

Dinner: 7.00 (you must bring your own wine)
Lunch: Not served
Breakfast: 8.15–9.00

Children: No

Dogs: In rooms only

Closed: November to early January

Directions: Arriving in Chagford from Eston or Sandy Park direction turn left in Chagford Square. Turn left at Globe Hotel and Bly House is second drive on right going out of village after the public car park

Special Features: Victoriana collection; Gardens leading on to moors
Croquet lawn

Price: £

HOTEL: Buildings♡ Rooms♥ Food♡ Garden♡ Views♡
AMENITIES: Riding♡ Croquet♥ Walks♥

If your idea of a romantic weekend is to spend it in a museum – Bly House will turn you on. Mr and Mrs Thompson have been collectors of Victoriana all their lives and it's all here for you to spend a few days in. Literally everything – from your breakfast cups to your bed – is real period stuff and, appropriately for the Victorian style, every corner of the house is crammed with pieces of china. Dogs and small children not encouraged!

The comfortable rooms lead on to a little sun terrace itself overlooking the gardens with wonderful views of the moors beyond. The house itself is a modest stone building – once Chagford Rectory – and built in about 1880.

The bedrooms are very romantic. Some have a four-poster or half-tester, and one has an exquisite single four-poster. All with chintzy-china antiques. The house is centrally heated.

Mrs Thompson's kitchen produces her personally home-cooked food. Much to our regret we were unable to stay but the sight of the meringues coming out of the Aga inspired confidence. The menu is simple and convincing – pork chop in ginger ale, red cabbage with orange. Mrs Thompson produces a menu a day and obviously loves every minute of it. It's all done in the Aga – the 'new' electric cooker has stood in the corner for some years with the wrapping paper still inside! Lots of ingredients are from Mr Thompson's vegetable garden and the house has its own spring water supply.

Warning: No wine! Bly house was bought from the Church with a 'no spiritous liquor' clause in the sale. This of course is a benefit to the serious wine drinkers who can bring whatever they want at no charge.

Mr and Mrs Thompson are a charming couple and very modest about their wonderful little hotel. You will have a quiet civilized stay amongst their regular clientele, enjoy the superb bedrooms, view and walks, and enjoy Mrs Thompson's fare in a delightful dining room with soft classical music to keep your amorous conversation private.

You will need to book in advance to ensure the four-posters.

Combe House Hotel

Combe House Hotel
Gittisham
Nr Honiton
Devon
EX14 OAD
Tel: Honiton (0404) 2756

Proprietors: John and Thérèse Boswell

Cards: All (deposit required with booking, confirmed in writing)

13 rooms (6 romantic, 3 with best views)

Dinner: 7.30–9.30
Lunch: Bar only during week, Sun: 1.00
Breakfast: 8.00–9.30

Children and dogs: Welcome

Open: Year-round

Directions: Off the A30 dual carriageway just outside Honiton towards Exeter sign posts to Hotel and Gittisham

Special Features: Beautiful views; Friendly and comfortable

Price: ££

HOTEL: Rooms♡ Food♡ Wine♡ Garden♡ Views♥
AMENITIES: Fishing♡ Walks♥

When John Boswell acquired the Combe House Hotel he determined to maintain as much as possible of the country-house atmosphere as would be consistent with running a comfortable and efficient hotel: in this he has been remarkably successful. The visitor enters into a splendid Caroline hall with dark panelling and a blazing fire on the hearth and, if he is sharp-eyed or particularly famished, he may spot a trolley laden with tempting sandwiches and cakes. The remaining reception rooms are attractive and well-furnished with a bar discreetly tucked off the end of one. The bedrooms are in the main original, disturbed as little as possible to accommodate bathrooms, and are well-equipped and comfortable with some fine furniture – those to the front elevation have magnificent views over the surrounding countryside. To welcome you – a nice touch – there is a jar of delicious homemade biscuits on the bedside table.

After a gigantic (and delicious) Kir Royale by the fire in the hall we dined by candlelight in one of the two adjacent dining rooms, each with its own attractive decorative scheme. The menu is small but selective with daily specialities: Lyme Bay lobster when we were there (which should be booked). The cooking is under the supervision of the owner's half-French wife so it is both well-prepared and elegantly presented: my Entrecôte grillé à la bearnaise, for example, was excellent, the beef tender, perfectly cooked and the slices separated by tranches of Beurre Maitre d'Hotel. The owners' son, when he is not attending food and wine courses – he had just returned from a stint in the kitchens of the Waterside Inn at Bray – also contributes. The wine list is well-selected and reasonably priced with a range of half-bottles and Muscat de Beaumes by the glass. The service was very friendly and relaxingly informal.

We much enjoyed our night at the Combe House Hotel to which the tranquillity and pleasure of the setting of the Devonshire countryside and the hospitality of Mr and Mrs Boswell contributed so much. After breakfast, chosen from a copious menu, we drove deeper into West Devon in the direction of Exeter and so were unable to see Lyme Regis – home of the 'French Lieutenant's Woman' and her creator – or any other of the many local places of interest.

Gidleigh Park

Gidleigh Park
Chagford
Devon
Tel: Chagford (06473) 2367

Owners: Paul and Kay Henderson

Cards: None but cheques in any currency, cash or Travellers' Cheques

12 rooms (all doubles)

Dinner: 7.00–9.00
Lunch: 12.30–1.30 by reservation; light lunch available anytime
Breakfast: Continental 7.30–10.30; Cooked 8.15–10.30

Children: Expected to behave as adults and charged accordingly

Dogs: Yes (rooms only)

Open: Year-round

Directions: Leave the A30 from Exeter for the A382 at Whiddon Down. At Easton turn right to Chagford. Turn right in the village at the square and fork right after 200 yards. At the crossroads go straight into Holly Street and follow for 1½ miles.

Special Features: Superb views and setting; Tasteful house and decor; Wine

Price: £££/££££

HOTEL: Buildings♥ Rooms♥ Food♥ Wine♥ Garden♥ Views♥
AMENITIES: Fishing♥ Golf♡ Riding♡ Croquet♥ Walks♥

The approach to Gidleigh Park must be one of the most romantic of all. One and a half miles of winding, single-lane track between Dartmoor walls and hedges, passing streams and woods. The house is in a magnificent setting. The large panelled lounge, dining room and bar with small conservatory all look out over the gardens falling to the stream and beyond to the hills of Dartmoor. These views are shared by most of the rooms, two of which have sizeable balconies ideal for summer breakfasts and romantic moonlit summer evenings.

The Hendersons' personal taste in furniture and decor achieves a comfortable serenity. Bedrooms and public spaces are furnished with antiques and chintz, but all with a lightness of touch and lots of flowers to achieve a spacious and airy atmosphere. The baths are in little alcoves – all very romantic – with real soaps, oils and shampoo, Royal Ascot white bathrobes and downlighting aimed at bringing out one's nicer features.

Gidleigh Park cuisine is sophisticated and creative. It is clear that no efforts are spared to get it right. Out turbot in lettuce with Pernod was beautiful. Honestly, for our taste some of the dishes are too rich but it must be said that the food at Gidleigh Park is widely acclaimed by knowledgeable critics and there is no doubt that if you appreciate elaborate and rich cuisine, you are unlikely to find better. Our desserts were superb. The service is personal and impeccable.

Gidleigh is rightly famous for its wine list – you should start reading it in the afternoon! Paul has selected lots of bargains but will help you make decisions about some serious clarets back to the 1930s. There is a very good range of '61s and '70s and an extensive American collection.

There are superb walks through lanes and fields and along the rivers. Dartmoor is extremely beautiful and our walks by blooming rhododendrons touching the river's edge, reflected in the water and backed by dense forest were unforgettable.

Gidleigh Park is rather grand. Its reputation is well-deserved. The standards are the highest but you will feel totally relaxed and at home because it all seems to be achieved so effortlessly. It isn't of course. It relies on a totally dedicated professionalism combined with the special taste and personal style of its owners.

This is the ideal place for the big romance. If you weren't sure about each other when you arrived – you will be madly in love by the time you leave.

Half Moon Inn

Half Moon Inn
Sheepwash
Devon
EX21 5NE
Tel: Black Torrington (040 923) 376

Owners: Charles and Benjie Inniss

Cards: Access, Barclaycard

14 rooms (9 with baths; 3 double beds)

Dinner: 8.00
Lunch: 12.00–1.45
Breakfast: 8.30–9.00

Children: Welcomed

Dogs: Allowed

Closed: 1 Nov–28 February (but open at w/e)

Directions: Take the A386 north from Okehampton to Hatherleigh, turn left on to the A3072 to Highampton then right for Sheepwash

Special Features: Fishing (salmon and trout); Traditional pub bar; Quiet village

Price: £

HOTEL: Buildings♡ Wine♡
AMENITIES: Fishing♥ Golf♡ Riding♡ Walks♥

The first thing you must remember about the Half Moon Inn is to take an Ordnance Survey Map. Without this you may not even find it and you certainly will miss many of the joys of the countryside walks from this out-of-the-way location.

The Inn forms one side of the Sheepwash village square next to the church tower. The square is the habitat of a lazy village dog unlikely to actually get on his feet until opening time, the occasional cow or two and not much else. It is amazingly peaceful.

The Half Moon Inn is first and foremost a fishing inn based on the excellent trout and salmon fishing on the nearby River Torridge. (Who says fishing isn't romantic!) Owners Charles and Benjie Inniss run this charming traditional inn now that their father has retired and visitors are welcomed as family guests. It is a fine example of an old country inn dating from Restoration times.

Entrance is through the wonderful and absolutely genuine village pub bar with its beams, flagstones, solid furniture and fishing memorabilia. The adjoining large dining room has antique dining tables laid in solid traditional and unpretentious style. A small lounge allows guests to escape the hubbub of the bar if they feel the need.

A traditional kitchen produces 'good home cooking' in English country style. There is a set menu each night and an excellent wine list of a hundred or so wines at very reasonable prices.

When everyone else is out during the day you will have the place to yourselves to be as romantic as you like. Bedrooms are plain and adequate, but not exciting like the rest of the inn. But if you are not fishing you will in any case be out exploring the wonderful surrounding countryside and following the Torridge up or down stream. This is a place for romantic walks and evenings in Benjie's bar meeting the locals and fishermen after dinner. They are all too busy telling fishing stories to notice what you are up to.

For those who want to fish Charles will see that you have everything you need and the latest information on where they are rising. Equipment can be rented or bought and there is a superb 'rod room' and drying facilities. Rates are about £4.50 a day for trout and £5.50 for salmon. Charles will provide tuition for beginners at £6.00 a lesson. You keep your catch!

Riverside

Riverside
Helford
Helston
Cornwall
Tel: Manaccan (032 623) 443

Resident owners: Heather Crosbie and George Perry-Smith

Cards: None

6 rooms (5 doubles, 1 twin)

Dinner: 7.30–9.30 (roughly)
Lunch: Light lunch on request
Breakfast: 8.30–9.30

Children: Accepted

Dogs: No

Directions: Leave Helston by the A3083 (direction Lizard). After 2½ miles turn left to Mawgan, Manaccan and Helford.

Special Features: Overlooking estuary; Small isolated village; Good food

Price: ££

HOTEL: Buildings♡ Food♥ Wine♥ Garden♡ Views♥
AMENITIES: Swimming♡ Fishing♡ Golf♡ Riding♡ Beach♡ Sailing♡

Riverside is owned and run by the charming Heather Crosbie and George Perry-Smith, previously of Hole in the Wall fame (Bath).

Helford is superbly isolated and has that 'end of the earth' feel about it. The road stops here. It is a tiny village formed on both banks of the small creek running into the Helford Estuary. Riverside itself has been formed from several of the little cottages on one bank. These are linked by little gardens, paths and steps.

The bedrooms, the dining room and a small drinks terrace look over the creek to cottages beyond. Apart from the few other cottages, Helford consists essentially of a Post Office, a charming pub, a couple of shops and a boat hire.

The approach to the village is through tall winding Cornish hedgerows that in spring and summer are a blaze of yellows, pinks and purples. This is not the Cornwall of bleak cliffs or moorland but of sheltered, tree-lined creeks and rivers, soft hedgerows and wild flowers.

Riverside is essentially a restaurant with a few beds and it is the kitchen that forms the heart of this unique hotel. From the time you wake to the smell of the croissants and brown bread rolls coming out of the oven, until the last sips of wine after dinner, it seems that all revolves around the kitchen. Far from being hidden away, the kitchen is the first thing you come to after the front gate. George and his young assistants can be seen and heard in busy enthusiastic preparation.

Heather will have seen that every available corner is occupied with those fresh hedgerow flowers and the whole place hums gently through the day until the great event of dinner. The food is excellent and the wine list extensive and affordable. A different menu is prepared each day and provides plenty of variety. We especially enjoyed the various hors d'oeuvres, the sweetbreads with sorrel and the brandade in puff pastry.

Helford is the place to do nothing and leave plenty of time to feel romantic. Finches and a robin will keep you company on the terrace as you relax. The rest of the world is a long way away.

Woodhayes

Woodhayes
Whimple
Nr Exeter
Devon
EX5 2TD
Tel: Whimple (0404) 822237

Proprietor: John Allan

Cards: AMX, Visa, Diners, Access

6 rooms (4 doubles, 2 twins)

Dinner: 8.00
Lunch: By arrangement if staying
Breakfast: Until 9.30

Children: No

Dogs: No

Open: Year-round

Directions: Take the A30 from Exeter towards Honiton, approx 9 miles. Whimple is signposted to the left, Woodhayes is just on the right after the 30mph sign

Special Features: Pretty countryside; Intimate charm

Price: £

HOTEL: Buildings♡ Rooms♡ Food♡ Wine♡ Garden♡ Views♡
AMENITIES: Walks♥

Woodhayes is on the edge of the village of Whimple in picturesque Devon, near Exeter. The hotel set in charming gardens is an 18th-century country-house with only six bedrooms.

John Allan, the proprietor, is there to meet you at the front door and shows you into the hall. He has been at Woodhayes for only 18 months since leaving his native Aberdeenshire and has already established an enviable reputation in the West Country. He is aided by a staff of three charming girls who are always keen to help in any way.

Our room was an example to all British hoteliers. The bed was a magnificent Victorian piece with crispy linen sheets, the dressing table had a fascinating selection of books ranging from *Treasure Island* to Nevil Shute. Attention to detail is John Allan's secret. We found the Malvern water on a silver salver in our room and the flowers were charming, but the bathroom was quite magnificent. Almost the same size as our room, it had huge towels, nice scented soaps and lead crystal glasses and even an armchair.

There are only six tables in the dining room, all laid with linen tablecloths, beautiful glasses and pretty plates and cutlery. The wine is left on the table in a silver coaster and John has a small but interesting wine list with a selection of unusual bin ends – we had a full bodied medium dry Bordeaux white. The menu is four-course and our starters were delicious: liver terrine and brioche of bacon and kidneys. The second course was a thick soup which in our case was crab bisque – delicious. The main course, a choice of four dishes was unusual showing a creative chef and we were even offered second helpings! Puddings included delicious homemade sorbets but one couldn't do justice to any of the other choices. Coffee and truffles are served in the drawing room.

We woke next morning to absolute silence and although breakfast would have been available in our room we went downstairs, finding our pre-ordered newspapers in our place. Breakfast was up to the high standards we had come to expect.

We didn't have time to play croquet on the lawns outside, but left feeling that we had found the ideal romantic hotel. For value, this is a hotel which takes some beating.

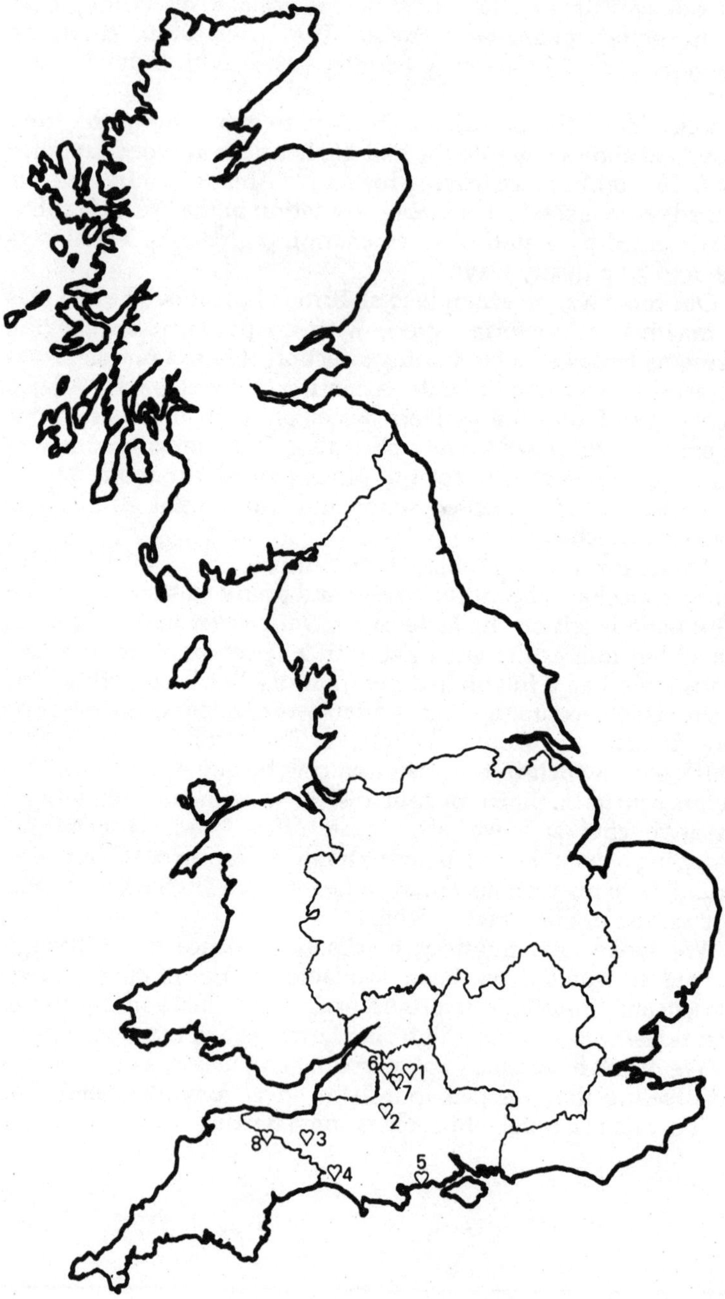

6
1
7
2
8
3
5
4

The South-West

1 Beechfield House, Beanacre, Wiltshire
2 Bishopstrow House, Warminster, Wiltshire
3 The Castle, Taunton, Somerset
4 Chedington Court, Beauminster, Dorset
5 Chewton Glen, New Milton, Hampshire
6 The Manor House, Castle Combe, Wiltshire
7 The Sign of the Angel, Lacock, Wiltshire
8 Tarr Steps Hotel, Hawkridge, Somerset

Beechfield

Beechfield House
Beanacre
Wilts
SN12 7PU
Tel: Melksham (0225) 703700

Resident Owners: Mr and Mrs Peter Crawford-Rolt

Cards: Amex, Diners, Visa, Access

16 rooms (4 doubles, 12 twins)

Dinner: 7.00–9.00 (later on Sat)
Lunch: 12.30–1.45
Breakfast: Continental 7.00–9.00

Children: Accepted if well-behaved

Dogs: No

Open: Year-round

Directions: Exit number 17 on the M4 and proceed due south to Laycock and Beanacre

Special Features: Very tastefully furnished (antiques); Heated swimming pool

Price: ££

HOTEL: Buildings♥ Rooms♥ Food♡ Wine♡ Garden♡ Views♡
AMENITIES: Tennis♥ Swimming♥ Fishing♡ Golf♡ Riding♡ Croquet♥ Walks♥

156

Beechfield is an ornate Victorian Bath Stone house set in several acres of mature gardens. A small terrace and rose garden separate the main building from the very well converted stable block which itself gives on to the terrace swimming pool.

Both buildings are charming and have stylish décor. The main house contains the public rooms with their antique furniture including many particularly lovely sofas. The two attractive dining rooms overlook the lawns. There is some beautiful Victorian stained glass and magnificent curtains everywhere. One room has a four-poster and all rooms are comfortable and attractive.

Mr and Mrs Crawford-Rolt are young and easy-going. You will feel immediately welcome and relaxed in the country house atmosphere they have created.

Peter supervises everything in the kitchen and, like the décor, the food is pretty and well-presented. We had a superb quail eggs and crab salad and a vegetable terrine in a fragrant tomato coulis followed by brill and scallops. The wine list provides an excellent range and good value at all prices – Peter Crawford-Rolt likes to see good wine being enjoyed rather than preserved and evidently a lot of his clientele are sympathetic to this.

Beanacre is not far from the beautiful National Trust village of Laycock and you can take a gentle evening stroll there by the footpath that follows the Avon – moonlight can sometimes be arranged.

On a summer evening you take your drink on the terrace or lawn – champagne or white wine in a silver cooler seems to go down best.

The owners certainly have got the idea of a relaxed, romantic hotel. We found ourselves sitting outside late after dinner, long after diners had dined and guests retired. The heated pool was still lit up and began to look extremely attractive. It was a summer night, there was nobody about so in we went 'au nature'. What a treat – and in the English countryside too!

We think you will enjoy Beechfield – even if it's too cold for swimming.

Bishopstrow House

Bishopstrow House
Warminster
Wilts
BA12 9HH
Tel: Warminster (0985) 212312

Resident Proprietors: The Schiller Family

Cards: American Express, Visa, Access

15 rooms: (2 apts, 7 doubles, 7 twins)

Dinner: 7.30–9.30
Lunch: 12.30–1.30
Breakfast: 8.00–9.30, English only in dining room

Children: None under 3

Dogs: By special arrangement

Closed: 3 weeks in January

Directions: Just outside Warminster on the A36 towards Salisbury

Special Features: Charming country house

Price: ££

HOTEL: Buildings♥ Rooms♥ Food♥ Wine♥ Garden♥ Views♡
AMENITIES: Tennis♥ Fishing♥ Golf♡ Riding♡ Croquet♥ Walks♡

Mr New the doorman welcomes you at your car when you arrive at Bishopstrow. The house has a quiet, relaxed elegance, being built in 1817 by John Pinch. The most spectacular bedroom is the 'Oval Room' at the top of the main staircase, but all the other rooms are comfortable, pretty and perfectly match the style of the house.

The spirit of the country-house pervades, with peacocks parading on the terraces and lawns with their mature cedar trees. However, the really romantic walk is through the tunnel under the road out into a secluded and beautiful garden. There you find an orchard and a little circular temple built in 1770 and nearby a pretty summer house overlooking the river. Here is a most perfect place to stroll and loiter beside the quiet little river. One of the most picturesque drives in England starts in Bishopstrow and follows the bottom of Wylye Valley down to Wilton.

Bishopstrow should be better known for its food. Mr Schiller and his chef Simon Collins are producing clever, sophisticated and unusual meals often, in the summer, enhanced by being served in the conservatory with its view of the garden.

Dinner really starts at a table in the inner hall or one of the reception rooms with a drink and a canape with the menu. You should take time to study and appreciate Mr Schiller's exceptional wine list. It has obvious stars: '61 Margaux, for instance, but all the clarets are either '70 or '75 and the burgundies equally impressive. The prices are near today's retail price (if you could buy them).

Care has been lavished on the dinner and the dining room. Each group eats at a slightly different time so that the chef can concentrate on each meal. When you are shown in, the wine will be in its coaster beside the folded napkin on a silver platter. The glasses are an unusual crystal. As suggested, I had a four-course dinner from their small menu of warm salad of pigeon, feullete aux fruits de mer, rack of lamb (perfectly pink in a jacket of herbs and breadcrumbs) and, finally, a liqueur soufflé.

This is the place for a quiet, romantic weekend with great food.

Castle Hotel

The Castle Hotel
Castle Green
Taunton
Somerset
TA1 1NF
Tel: Taunton (0823) 72671
Telex: 46488

Owner/manager: Kit Chapman

Credit cards: Access, Amex, Diners, Visa

40 rooms (3 double bedrooms, but all twin rooms have special 3′ 6″ beds; 'Bow Suite', Nos 58, 61, 65, and 111 recommended)

Dinner: 7.30–9.30
Lunch: 12.30–2.00

Breakfast: 7.45–10.00

Children: Accepted (but disciplined about dining room behaviour!)

Dogs: In rooms only

Open: Year-round

Directions: In centre of town, part of the Castle

Special Features: Part of original Taunton Castle; Secluded Norman garden; Good romantic touring base; Winter-weekend festivals (fine wine, music and theatre)

Price: £££

HOTEL: Buildings♥ Rooms♥ Food♥ Wine♥ Garden♡
AMENITIES: Tennis♡ Golf♡ Riding♡

Taunton is an excellent base for explorations of the romantic West Country and the Castle Hotel is certainly the most romantic place to stay. You have your choice of Lorna Doone's Exmoor, King Arthur's Glastonbury or Thomas Hardy country (or you can play at being Meryl Streep on the harbour wall at Lyme Regis!).

Kit Chapman and his attentive staff will be pleased to point you in the right direction. (They have even prepared a few romantic tour handouts with suggestions of where to lunch and drink during the day.) Back at the Hotel the romance continues. The atmosphere is established, traditional and immensely warm and welcoming.

Many of the rooms are decorated in a light-hearted romantic way – some with antique boudoir furniture and some with a colonial feel with light wood beds and large birds or flower patterned materials. Ask for a 'romantic room' when you book – Kit or his general manager David Prior will know exactly what you mean. Little bouquets and welcome notes with miniature sherries, a few silk-covered padded hangers for evening dresses and various other touches are all noticeable.

The Castle does not have extensive rural views – it's in the town. It does have, however, a wonderful little Norman garden with pretty nooks and crannies where you can take your summer drinks. In spring the wistaria covers the whole four-storey building and creeps into your bedroom window. It's the oldest and most romantic wistaria in England according to Kit Chapman (for whom the idea of the Romantic Weekend Book needed no further explanation!).

The food at the Castle is some of the best we have had. Chris Oakes has a style that is creative, fresh and not over-powering. We had a fresh asparagus with warm chicken livers and peeled grapes (very sensual!) followed by a salmon steak on leaf spinach with a fresh tarragon and butter sauce (irresistible!). You will be completely seduced by the veal in creamed leek sauce. We were tempted (and succumbed!) to taste a bilberry coulis with sliced poached pear which was a nectar and (decadent!) chocolate marquise on a delicious coffee bean sauce. The dining atmosphere is all good solid castle stuff with plain white tablecloths, plates and icebuckets. Leave lots of time for your romantic dinner – some of the most interesting choices take 25 minutes to assemble – and relish the anticipation.

Chedington Court

Chedington Court
Chedington
Beaminster
Dorset
DT8 3HY
Tel: Corscombe (093589) 265

Resident owners: Hilary and Philip Chapman

Cards: Amex

8 rooms (3 doubles, 5 twins; one four-poster)

Dinner: 7.00–9.15
Lunch: Not normally done
Breakfast: As ordered

Children: Accepted

Dogs: No

Open: Year-round

Directions: Leave the A30 at Crewkerne. Take the A356 (direction Dorchester). Chedington is 5 miles on the right.

Special Features: Beautiful gardens; Victorian conservatory; Views (Hardy country); Helicopter landing

Price: £/££ (good bargain breaks)

HOTEL: Buildings♥ Rooms♡ Food♡ Wine♥ Garden♥ Views♥
AMENITIES: Tennis♡ Fishing♡ Golf♡ Riding♡ Croquet♥ Walks♡

Chedington Court is a Jacobean style manor house built in the 1840s on the site of the ancient Chedington estate. It is attractive inside and out and its stone mullioned windows command wonderful views of the grounds and beyond to the Dorset countryside.

The grounds are some of the best owned by a hotel anywhere and typically English. Terraces overlook the croquet lawn and wistaria climbs up to the stone balustrades. Large ponds set in extensive lawns form changes of level and eventually the overflow falls to a small river among flowers, plants and stones.

Extensive topiary contains lawned spaces and ancient gravestones mark the site of the old church within the estate – also rebuilt in the 1840s and now hidden in the trees overlooking Chedington's grounds.

Within all this, Hilary and Philip Chapman create a relaxed and informal atmosphere for your romantic stay. There are only eight rooms, so you often have the place to yourselves. You can wander about, hold hands in the gardens under the high, mature cedars or sit in the little summer house watching the ducks. Although the setting is grand, there is a delightful casualness about the place. You can trip over the watering can in the conservatory (which has just the right amount of peeling paint and two or three panes missing!), help yourself to a garden chair and discover the croquet set whilst about it. The owners are there if you call – but not if you don't.

Hilary Chapman supervises all in the kitchen and produces an interesting fixed menu freshly prepared each evening. (The Chapmans ran Oaklands at South Petherton for seven years before opening Chedington in 1981.) We had a spinach-filled crêpe, a wonderful salmon with velouté sauce and a fillet of beef. Desserts are very good – including a secret orange pie. The wine list is extensive and provides a wide choice of sensibly priced wines from almost everywhere you are likely to want to try wine from (the ducks are reputed to live in a Château Latour case!)

The Victorian conservatory is a great asset and enables you to sip your morning coffee or evening drink outside during many months of the year. If you time your visit right, you can sit under the mimosa or the passion flowers.

All the main bedrooms are huge and most have nice features and great views.

Wind up your evening with a stroll in the gardens under the high trees against the sky, with the house lights burning in the drawing room, the conservatory lighting up the terraced lawns ... and your romantic weekend is beginning.

Chewton Glen

Chewton Glen Hotel
New Milton
Hants
BH25 6QS
Tel: Highcliffe (04252) 5341
Telex: 41456

Owner: Martin Skan and family

Cards: All

50 rooms (40 doubles, 2 singles, 8 suites; two bathrooms have whirlpool baths)

Dinner: 7.30–9.30 (private dining room seating up to 20 available)
Breakfast: 7.00–9.45
Lunch: 12.30–2

Children: Over 7

Dogs: No

Open: Year-round

Directions: On A337 between Highcliffe and Lymington. Do *not* follow signs for New Milton; look for signs to Highcliffe

Special Features: Superb food and wine; Several rooms and suites have private patios

Price: £££/££££

HOTEL: Buildings♡ Rooms♥ Food♥ Wine♥ Garden♥ Views♡
AMENITIES: Tennis♥ Swimming♥ Fishing♡ Golf♡ Riding♡ Beach♡ Sailing♡ Croquet♥ Walks♥

Chewton Glen is the Rolls-Royce of country-house hotels. It is luxurious, timeless and functions with unobtrusive efficiency. Such perfection commands a high price, for which you expect the best of everything – and get it.

From the moment when your car is parked and luggage carried to your room, the staff of Chewton Glen (who almost outnumber the guests) will look after you, combining friendliness with discreet and impeccable service. Your room may be in the grand Georgian mansion, where Captain Marryat was inspired to write his classic novel *The Children of the New Forest*, or in the adjoining beautifully converted coach house.

Each room is individually decorated with emphasis on comfort. Many have private terraces where you can sip the sherry which awaits your arrival or enjoy your delicious breakfast, enveloped in a fluffy bathrobe. If you feel like mingling, there are several attractive bars and drawing-rooms where comfortable chairs are covered in bright fabrics and leather-bound books fill the alcoves.

Chewton Glen is deservedly famous for its restaurant and magnificent wine list. The food is imaginative and pleases all the senses; the best ingredients superbly prepared and beautifully presented on fine china, in a spacious and elegant dining room – a gourmet's paradise. It is typical of Chewton Glen that their petit-fours (homemade, of course) are served in a lavish basket that is itself made of sugar.

In fine weather you can lunch outdoors on one of the terraces, sunbathe by the beautiful pool, walk across the fields to the sea or ride in the New Forest but, whatever the weather, there's plenty to do. If you need pampering in supremely comfortable surroundings, look no further then Chewton Glen.

The Manor House

The Manor House
Castle Combe
Chippenham
Wilts
SN14 7HR
Tel: Castle Combe (0249) 782206
Telex: 44220

Proprietor: Mr O. R. Clegg

Cards: All

33 rooms (13 in main building, 4 four-posters; 29 doubles in all)

Dinner: 7.30–9.00
Lunch: 12.30–2.00
Breakfast: 8.00–9.30

Children: Welcome

Dogs: Welcome

Open: Year-round

Special Features: Very pretty village; Lovely grounds with river

Price: ££

HOTEL: Buildings♥ Rooms♡ Food♡ Wine♡ Garden♥
AMENITIES: Swimming♡ Golf♡ Riding♡

Out of the flat and rather dull countryside round Chippenham, the road to Castle Combe dips unexpectedly into a thickly wooded valley with a rich carpet of flowers beneath the trees. Castle Combe itself is a magical stone village apparently untouched by time. At the end of the village lies the entrance to the Manor House past a row of cottages with front doors directly on the street which have been ingeniously converted into an annexe. The first impression as you enter through the gates is the ever-present sound of water from the weir across the River Bibrock which winds through the 26 acres of beautiful grounds.

The Manor House is originally 17th century with many later additions, though an earlier Manor claimed Sir John Fastolf as lord, reputedly the model for Shakespeare's anti-hero. The public rooms are very comfortable and well-appointed: there is a very cosy panelled bar where orders are taken for dinner and the dining room itself, a relatively recent addition, is on a grand scale. Our table was by one of the windows and while we dined we could watch the twilight deepening over the enclosed parkland outside. The menu both table d'hôte and à la carte was extensive and the food good and very prettily presented. There is a wide and well-priced wine list with some exciting varieties for those with well-lined pockets!

We were very comfortable in our room in the annexe which, like all rooms, was pleasantly furnished, but the overwhelming impressions of our stay were the extreme peace and beauty of the setting. The old trees, the steeply sloping Italian garden with its crumbling folly atop, the constant music of the River and, indeed, the village itself make the valley a quite exceptionally calm and sequestered spot to spend a weekend while the Manor House sees charmingly and competently to the creature comforts. And, if you do tear yourself away for a time, there is much to see in the area and in the general direction of Bath more good eating is to be had.

Sign of the Angel

Sign of the Angel
Lacock
Nr Chippenham
SN15 2LB
Tel: Lacock (024 973) 230

Owners: Mr and Mrs John Levis

Cards: None

6 rooms (4 doubles)

Dinner: 7.30–8.00

Children: By appointment

Dogs: Only well-behaved

Closed: 22 December – 1 January

Special Features: 15th-century wool merchant's house; Fox Talbot museum; Lacock Abbey; Antique furniture; National Trust village

Price: ££

HOTEL: Buildings♥ Rooms♥ Food♡ Wine♡
AMENITIES: Walks♥

In the 15th-century the Sign of the Angel was a wool merchant's house. Now it is a delightful, traditional village inn with head-banging beams, oak panelling and sloping doors and floors. The pretty little upstairs lounge has a working stone fireplace, soft lighting and comfortable armchairs. Mr and Mrs John Levis and son John run this cosy restaurant with six rooms in an altogether informal and comfortable fashion.

All the rooms have appropriate antique furniture, including squeaky armchairs. The wonderful ornate carved Spanish double bed in room No. 3 was particularly difficult to resist after our lunch.

The two dining rooms have a lovely collection of spacious dining tables – no two the same – and are nicely but informally laid with mixed silver plate, flowers and plain glass creating a solid but unpretentious feel. We would have appreciated proper rather than paper serviettes. The food, too, is simple. Ingredients are fresh and dishes traditional with good solid terrines and roasts. Our beef was slightly overcooked for our French taste, but the Yorkshire pudding was a treat. Good plain fresh vegetables. We had an excellent homemade strawberry ice cream and a rich creme caramel. Desserts will be served before cheese unless you ask! Plenty of wonderful fresh cream available from the family cow. The wine list provides adequate choice without involving a major read, and most regions are represented.

Sign of the Angel is a low-key, relaxed, family-run inn housed in a superb historic building that is maintained in its original form. It's more like a private house than a hotel. You will feel welcome and enjoy a quiet English village weekend.

Lacock itself is a charming well preserved National Trust village. Be sure to leave time to visit the Fox Talbot museum of early photographs and Lacock Abbey.

Tarr Steps

Tarr Steps Hotel
Hawkridge
Nr Dulverton
Somerset
Tel: Winsford (064 385) 293 Reception; 218 Guests

Resident Proprietors: Desmond and Rupert Keane

Cards: AMX and Visa; cheques preferred (if booking, send deposit)

15 rooms (7 doubles, 2 four-posters (Nos. 3 and 14), 5 twins)

Dinner: 8.00
Lunch: Bar or packed available
Breakfast: 8.30–9.45 English breakfast in dining room only

Children: Welcome

Dogs: Welcome

Open: 1 March – 3 January

Directions: Take the Hawkridge road north out of Dulverton (off the B3222). At Five Crosses go right. At Hawkridge keep on the road (left opposite the church) to Tarr Steps. The Hotel is at the end of the road.

Special Features: The countryside; Views, walks, fishing; Stables for your own horses

Price: £

HOTEL: Food♡ Wine♡ Garden♡ Views♥
AMENITIES: Fishing♥ Riding♥ Walks♥

The approach to Tarr Steps gave us wonderful views from the wild top of Exmoor with new-born lambs frolicking beside the road, then suddenly we found ourselves in amongst the trees of a little wooded valley with a trout stream rushing along beside us. The Hotel is literally at the end of the road near a ford crossed by a Bronze Age footbridge, built with ancient huge slabs of stone.

We had had a wet and cold drive but we had an immediate welcome by the fire in the bar and a great pot of tea and homemade fruit cake. The Hotel used to be the rectory for a sporting parson and this feeling of solid Victorian comfort reigns throughout: brass glints and sporting prints abound. The place has a warm Mrs Tiggiwinkle atmosphere which is a bright haven from one's exertions in the countryside all around.

Tarr Steps casts its spell through its setting of unadulterated wild countryside. We remember the walks in the woods and across the moors with the sound of rushing water and the sight of a heron flapping away in fright, or the deer silhouetted on the far hill during dinner.

Guests sit down to dinner with a candle burning and their own damask napkin in its silver ring beside them. The light is soft in the dark green room with its pictures of the owners' ancestors on the walls. The food is good French-style English cooking produced by the Cordon Bleu trained cook. We had beefsteak braised in Guinness and port. The breakfasts are magnificent and set you up for the day.

On Sundays there is clay-shooting followed by a proper Sunday lunch which leaves you ready to return to the big city; only about 3½ hours to London or the Midlands.

The Tarr Steps Hotel is a real get-away-from-it-all place. The guests are all united in one thing: they love the countryside. We would recommend it, for its location alone. It is the perfect place to propose – on a walk by the river. Mr Keane, the owner, keeps a bottle of vintage and non-vintage champagne in the fridge for celebrations.

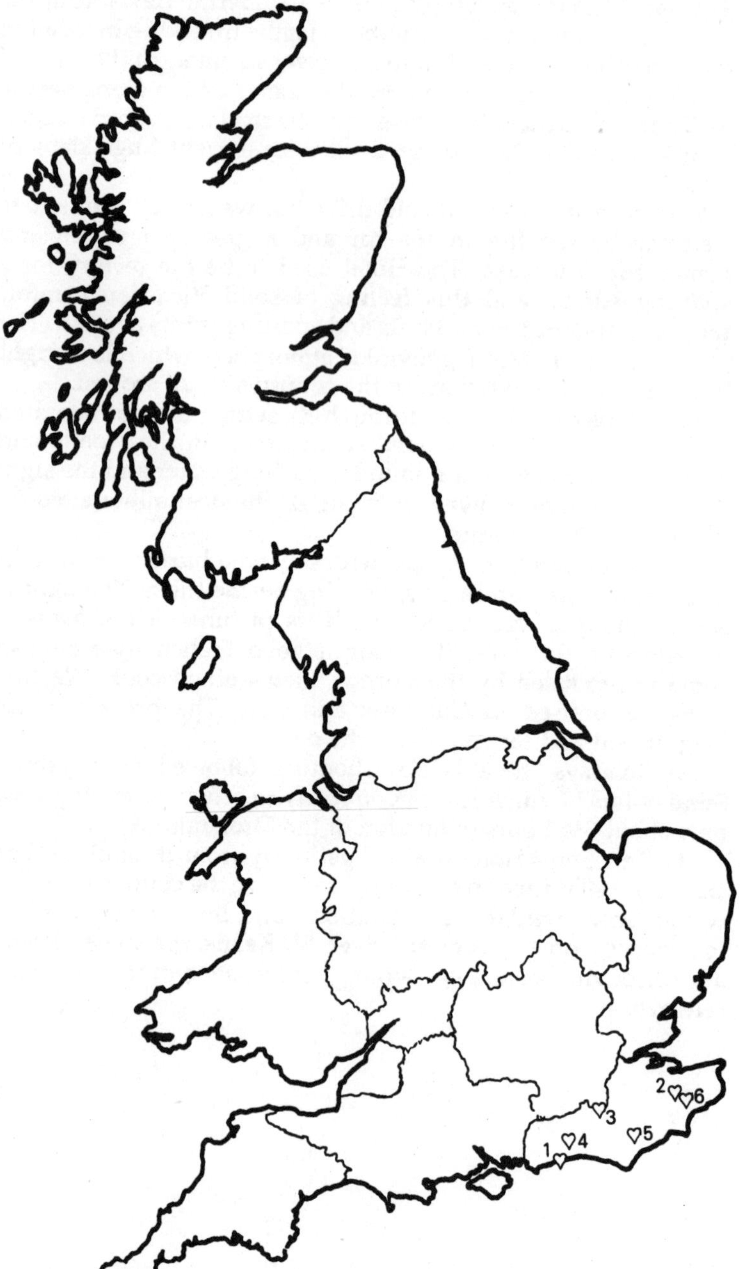

2
6
3
5
4
1

Sussex and Kent

1. Bailiffscourt Hotel, Climping, W. Sussex
2. Eastwell Manor, Ashford, Kent
3. Gravetye Manor, East Grinstead, E. Sussex
4. Little Thakeham, Storrington, W. Sussex
5. The Priory, Rushlake Gren, E. Sussex
6. Stone Green Hall, Mersham, Kent

Bailiffscourt

Bailiffscourt Hotel
Climping
Littlehampton
W. Sussex
BN17 5RW
Tel: Littlehampton (09064) 23511

Owner: Mrs Julia Hoskins

Cards: All major accepted

18 rooms (15 doubles – 6 with four-posters, 7 with open fires; 3 suites)

Dinner: 7.30–10.00
Lunch: 12.30–2.00
Breakfast: 7.30–10.30

Children: No

Dogs: £3.45 per night

Open: Year-round except January

Directions: Off A259 between Littlehampton and Bognor Regis

Special Features: Reconstructed medieval house; Sauna and exercise rooms

Price: £££

HOTEL: Buildings♥ Rooms♥ Wine♡ Garden♥ Views♡
AMENITIES: Tennis♥ Swimming♥ Golf♡ Riding♡ Beach♡ Sailing♡ Croquet♥ Walks♡

Secluded on the coast near Arundel, Bailiffscourt is literally a dream come true. Less than 50 years ago this perfect re-creation of a medieval house was constructed to satisfy the whim of the late Lord Moyne, using beautiful stone, beams, windows and doors from derelict medieval buildings throughout Britain. The result is a 'genuine fake', and the perfect setting for making your own dreams into reality.

The golden stone walls, several feet thick, envelop you with a sense of tranquillity as you arrive and the courteous receptionist calls for someone to carry your luggage. Along stone-flagged passages, up flights of stairs, and a gnarled oak door is thrown open to reveal your comfortable room furnished, it seems, with genuine medieval objects (though these, too, are brilliant fakes). All the rooms are peaceful and each has its own character; thoughtful touches include fresh flowers, delicious biscuits, and even dog baskets. The bathrooms are splendid too, with generously proportioned 1930's fittings, sweet-smelling soap and bubblebath and luxurious towels and bathrobes. Room No. 22 costs more than the others but with good reason: it is immense and the four-poster bed seems large enough for six people. Candles on the bedside tables and a log fire cast flickering light over the medieval roof beams. There are *two* baths in the spacious bathroom, though you may end up sharing one. What could be more romantic than waking in this vast room as dappled sunlight filters through the mullioned windows and a peacock calls from the lawn?

In fine weather you can have drinks or lunch in the courtyard round which the house is built and then wander in the well-kept gardens, talk to the Welsh ponies which the owner breeds, walk through the fields down to the beach or swim in the hotel's own pool. If it's wet, enjoy the sauna, play table-tennis or cards, or curl up by one of the many fires with a good book. This beautiful house in its tranquil grounds offers a romantic setting that's hard to beat.

Eastwell Manor

Eastwell Manor
Eastwell Park
Ashford
Kent
TN25 4HR
Tel: Ashford (0233) 35751
Telex: 966281

Managers: Francis and Anja Stileman

Cards: All

21 rooms (6 twins, 15 doubles)

Dinner: 7.30–9.30
Lunch: 12.30–2.00 (special Sun lunch)
Breakfast: 7.30–9.30 (English served in rooms)

Children: Not in restaurant

Dogs: No

Open: Year-round

Directions: Take the A251 Faversham Road out of Ashford. Eastwell Manor is a few miles on left-hand side.

Special Features: Excellent food

Price: £££

HOTEL: Food♥ Wine♥ Garden♡ Views♡
AMENITIES: Tennis♥ Golf♡ Riding♡ Walks♥

Eastwell Manor is for gastronome romantics. The restaurant merits a star in the *Michelin Guide* which puts it among the few hotels in England to have that accolade. The chef, Ian McAndrew, is one of the young men from this side of the Channel who is leading the quiet revolution for the new and creative cuisine being increasingly enjoyed in England.

The setting is a grey stone Elizabethan-style house built in the 1920s, flanked by two walled gardens, within the boundary of a previous house looking out on to the pretty Kent countryside. The interior is ponderous with heavy leather Chesterfields in rooms with dark oak panelling.

Dinner was the zenith of our visit. We were professionally guided through the menu and the impressive wine list. We opted for the very reasonably priced (£20.00) 'Menu Degustation'. The rules for eating this are: no lunch and you must order before 9.00. It consists of seven courses and would have appealed enormously to King Edward VII who once stayed here, with its sorbet to whet the palate for the beef. It was as follows: foie gras sauté au poire pochée, crème au lait d'amandes, St Pierre poché aux mousserons, sorbet de citron vert, pavé de boeuf au cölis de Navets, beignets de figues au sabayon de Porto, café et chocolats maison.

The bedrooms are provided with every comfort – bathrobes, full sized colour TV, fruit and Malvern water in the room. The receptionist calls you soon after your arrival, to organize a time for dinner, your choice of breakfast (full English is available in your room with marmalade made in the kitchens) and your paper for the next morning. Romantics must stay in the 'Countess of Middleton' suite with its vast rooms and the original Edwardian bath and shower – no drizzle, but a proper drenching.

Gravetye Manor

Gravetye Manor
Nr East Grinstead
E. Sussex
RH19 4LJ
Tel: Sharpthorne (0342) 810567
Telex: 957239

Proprietor: Peter Herbert

Manager: Helmut Kircher

Cards: None

14 rooms (12 doubles)

Dinner: 7.30–9.30
Lunch: 12.30–2.00
Breakfast: 8.00–10.00 (full English served in room – recommended)

Children: Not under 7

Dogs: No

Open: Year-round

Directions: From London take A22 just outside E. Grinstead, go right at a roundabout (spire of Mormon temple on right) on to the B2110 to Turners Hill. Drive about 2 miles then follow the signs for Gravetye Manor.

Special Features: Wonderful cuisine; Pretty house; Lovely gardens

Price: £££

HOTEL: Buildings♥ Rooms♡ Food♥ Wine♥ Garden♥ Views♥
AMENITIES: Fishing♡ Golf♡ Riding♡ Croquet♥ Walks♥

Gravetye Manor stands in the middle of a forest. When a golden pheasant sauntered in front of my car in the drive this was certainly a good omen, reinforced by a notice saying 'Flowers dislike exhaust fumes please park head on'. You arrive to find a pretty house covered in creeper surrounded by the beautiful gardens. The porch welcomes you with an arrangement of flowers and just off it a selection of Wellington boots to explore the garden in wet weather. This is exactly what the spirit of a country-house hotel should be, which isn't surprising as Peter Herbert opened Gravetye in 1957 and is one of the founders of the movement.

We were ushered into the panelled drawing room where in winter a huge wood fire blazes, but when we visited the door was open to a little walled garden with the scent of flowers and bird songs drifting into this quiet and dignified room.

The food at Gravetye is of simple excellence: we had an unusual and delicious home-smoked duck breast and one of their specialities, 'Salmon trout Beaulieu', with a nice white burgundy from their very good wine list. A charming touch is the Gravetye spring water culled from a spring in the grounds which is automatically served chilled in the restaurant and kept in a thermos in each of the rooms.

The rooms are comfortable country house bedrooms with all those nice touches which make all the difference: special soap, fresh flowers and a TV with remote control. Beside the bed, amongst other books is a book about William Robinson, the great gardener who lived at Gravetye and created the famous gardens. Lawns stretch out from the back of the house with a terrace where we had a drink admiring the profusion of flowering shrubs and dipping swallows in the evening air. We wandered out to the gazebo and watched the sun set over the lake in the little wooded valley. After dinner we went out again for a moonlight stroll down the wooded walks and amongst the high rhododendron bushes.

This quiet idyllic setting with superb food and great comfort makes Gravetye the perfect place for a romantic weekend.

Little Thakeham

Little Thakeham
Merrywood Lane
Storrington
W. Sussex
RH20 3HE
Tel: Storrington (09066) 4416

Proprietors: Tim and Pauline Ratcliff

Cards: All

8 rooms (3 doubles, 4 twins)

Dinner: 7.30–9.30
Lunch: 1.00–2.30 by arrangement
Breakfast: When you wake up

Children: Welcome

Dogs: No

Open: Year-round except Christmas

Directions: Take the A24 south from Horsham past Ashington, turn right towards Thakeham. Before Thakeham right on to Merrywood Lane. Little Thakeham is on right-hand side

Special Features: House and furniture by Sir Edward Lutyens; Superb views

Price: £££

HOTEL: Buildings♥ Rooms♥ Food♥ Wine♥ Garden♥ Views♥
AMENITIES: Tennis♥ Swimming♥ Golf♡ Riding♡ Croquet♥ Walks♥

Little Thakeham was built for a family of five and thirteen servants and it is not difficult to see why its original owner was bankrupted soon after its completion. The building, one of the finest examples of Sir Edward Lutyens's style, evokes an Elizabethan manor house and contains many examples of original Lutyens furniture. With its gardens designed by Gertrude Jekyll, a visit to Little Thakeham is all period charm with its unspoiled elegance.

Tim and Pauline Ratcliff bought the house four years ago and have created a unique hotel which soon puts you under its spell. The conversion from house to hotel has been cleverly achieved with excellent taste and minimum alterations; the new bathrooms reflect the architectural mood of the house with their oak bath surrounds and original doors with steel and brass fittings.

If you wish to sleep in a Lutyens bed, choose the 'Chanctonbury Suite' or, if you fancy a magnificent fireplace with candles over it and the typical Lutyens herringbone brick pattern, opt for the 'Library Suite'. Honeymoon couples are usually given the 'Mistress Suite', but do not expect pink and frills, even here all the bedrooms are decorated in keeping with the style of the house.

On an almost perfect evening we strolled in the garden with its paved walks, passed under the scented rose pergola and admired the views over acres of farmland and orchards. Sipping a glass of champagne in the bar, we ordered dinner and selected our wine from the very comprehensive wine list. The food is traditional English and French haute cuisine and full advantage is taken of local produce. We began with the mushrooms farcie and the avocado with smoked salmon mousse and followed with one roast rack of Southdown lamb (a speciality) with rosemary and garlic and the breast of duck with Little Thakeham plum sauce. The peach and brandy cheesecake and a chocolate mousse completed an excellent dinner.

The hotel is run very much like a private house, service is efficient yet purposely unobtrusive to ensure privacy. Meal times are flexible and late arrivals are always catered for; breakfast is when you wake up which is lovely. The relaxed atmosphere achieved together with the inherent charm of the surroundings make Little Thakeham an almost perfect weekend retreat.

The Priory Country House

The Priory Country House Hotel
Rushlake Green
Heathfield
Sussex
TN21 9RG
Tel: Rushlake Green (0435) 830553

Owners: Jane and Peter Dunn

Cards: None

Deposit: Advance booking (deposit required)

12 rooms (11 doubles, 6 in main house, 6 in converted byre)

Dinner: 7.30–9.00
Lunch: 12.30–2.00 (must book)
Breakfast: 8.30–9.30 (Continental in rooms), English in dining room till 9.45, early morning tea from 8.10)

Children: None under 9

Dogs: Not in public rooms

Open: 16 January–22 December

Directions: Take A 265 east out of Heathfield. Right on B2096 towards Battle. Right to Rushlake Green. The Priory is on the left fork of the road approaching the village

Special Features: Converted priory; Pretty countryside

Price: ££

HOTEL: Buildings♥ Rooms♡ Food♡ Wine♡ Garden♡ Views♡
AMENITIES: Croquet♥ Walks♡

The approach to the Priory is by a long drive between the fields in the prettiest part of the cosy rolling Sussex countryside. The old Priory dating from the 15th century has been in the Dunn family for generations as a farmhouse, but when the last tenant left they decided to create a hotel. It was a massive job to maintain the character of the place with its huge stone block walls and half timbering and yet meet all the fire regulations. The Dunns had never run a hotel before so the whole place reflects a fresh personal character which has founded their reputation.

You are made immediately welcome in the hall with its sofas set in front of an enormous blazing log fire. The bedrooms reflect the pretty farmhouse feeling with their simple whitewashed walls, oak timbers, and leaded panes offset by the chintz curtains with their matching bedspreads and hot water bottle covers laid out on the bed. Our room was decorated with a nice flower arrangement made up of flowers from the garden and wild flowers, prints of fruit on the wall and a couple of hand-painted plates on a shelf. The bathroom had that touch we particularly appreciate of two different soaps, violet and sweet-pea.

Particular effort has been taken with the food prepared by Cindy Parrot in the original kitchens. We had sweetbread and spinach terrine with a fresh ginger sauce followed by guinea fowl with a sherry vinegar sauce, then a black currant soufflé and a selection of cheeses from their excellent board. The wine list is particularly interesting as it was compiled by Nicholas Clarke, a wine master, which gives a good introduction to all the wines. However, the most important point is that the hotel has a policy of putting the same mark-up on all bottles so that the more expensive wines become very good value.

The Priory is definitely a place to relax in comfort and perhaps visit Glyndebourne: they provide sensational picnics.

Stone Green Hall

Stone Green Hall
Mersham
Nr Ashford
Kent
Tel: Aldington (0233 72) 418

Resident Proprietors: Ingrid and James Kempston

Cards: Access, Visa, AMX (with reluctance)

4 rooms (all doubles; master bedroom and 'Blue Room' have baths en suite)

Dinner: 7.30–9.30
Lunch: By arrangement
Breakfast: When you wake up, English downstairs

Children: Not under 12
Dogs: No

Directions: Take the A20 south from Ashford. About 2 miles from Ashford, right to Mersham through the village turn right at junction to Aldington. Go another mile past cricket pitch on left is the Hall.

Special Features: Lovely house; Informal intimacy

Price: £

HOTEL: Buildings♥ Rooms♥ Food♡ Wine♡ Garden♥ Views♡
AMENITIES: Tennis♥ Fishing♡ Golf♡ Riding♡ Croquet♥ Walks♥

You are always overwhelmed when your expectations are shattered by something far better than your wildest dreams. Here in the middle of rural Kent is a perfect early Georgian house built round the core of an older Cromwellian cottage. You are welcomed in the Hall with its polished wood floor and unusual stairs, but quickly whisked through the restaurant into the conservatory, an unexpected curved space reminiscent of Kew with its bougainvilleas in bloom, camellias in mid-winter and a hedge of hibiscus. Here a cool drink is quickly thrust into your hand.

The house is the home of Ingrid and James Kempston who decided four years ago to give up his job as a printer. He had always enjoyed cooking and on visiting the Dupays' Priory realized he wanted to do something like it. Here is the dream come true.

The dinner we enjoyed was superb: fresh English asparagus, salmon with an exquisite sorrel sauce, raspberry and framboise eau de vie sorbet, a salad of eclectic greeneries from the garden including baby broad bean leaves, a choice of two perfectly ripe French cheeses and, finally, some strawberries with a glass of Beaumes de Venise. We ate in the conservatory which is a magnificent setting for a warm summer night, looking beyond the ha-ha at the sheep grazing in the meadow. The garden is divided up with huge 20-foot high yew hedges, some hiding the gazebo reflected in the little pond, others harbouring the croquet lawn and grass tennis court.

Stone Green Hall is a special treat for it only has four bedrooms but these are magnificent and as beautiful as anything we have seen anywhere. They were originally decorated by Colefax and Fowler but they now have that personal charm added by the Kempstons. They even have little refrigerators hidden in the fireplace cupboard keeping a half bottle of champagne chilled. One room has a four-poster bath! Of course, staying at Stone Green Hall is like being part of an informal house party at a very sumptuous country-house. There are no times for breakfast: it's when you wake up or get up.

Here is something very special, charming and extraordinarily romantic. We cannot wait to stay again.

Index by Hotel

The Abbey Hotel, Penzance, Cornwall   140
Ardanaiseig, Kilchrenan, Scotland   18
Bailiffscourt Hotel, Climping, Sussex   174
Beechfield House, Beanacre, The South-West   156
Bell Inn, Aston Clinton, London & Home Counties   106
Bishopstrow House, Warminster, The South-West   158
Blakes, London, London & Home Counties   108
Bly House, Chagford, Devon   142
Bodysgallen Hall Hotel, Llandudno, Wales   50
Buckland Manor, Buckland, The Cotswolds   74
The Castle Hotel, Taunton, The South-West   160
Chedington Court, Beaminster, The South-West   162
Chewton Glen Hotel, New Milton, The South-West   164
The Clifton Hotel, Nairn, Scotland   20
The Close at Tetbury, Tetbury, The Cotswolds   76
Combe House Hotel, Gittisham, Devon   144
Congham Hall, Grimston, East Anglia   126
The Cottage in the Wood, Malvern Wells, Central England   60
Cromlix House, Dunblane, Scotland   22
The Crown at Whitebrook, Whitebrook, Wales   52
Dormy House, Broadway, The Cotswolds   78
Eastwell Manor, Ashford, Kent   176
11 Cadogan Gardens, London, London & Home Counties   110
The French Horn, Sonning-on-Thames, London & Home Counties   112
The Gentle Gardener, Tetbury, The Cotswolds   80
Gidleigh Park, Chagford, Devon   146
Gravetye Manor, East Grinstead, Sussex   178
The Greenway, Shurdington, The Cotswolds   82
Greywalls, Gullane, Scotland   24
Half Moon Inn, Sheepwash, Devon   148
Hall Garth Country House, Coatham Mundeville, The North   36
Hambleton Hall, Oakham, Central England   62
Homewood Park, Hinton Charterhouse, Avon   94
Hope End Country House, Ledbury, Central England   64
Hunstrete House Hotel, Hunstrete, Avon   96
Inverlochy Castle, Fort William, Scotland   26
Isle of Eriska, Ledaig, Scotland   28

Johnstounburn House, Humbie, Scotland 30
Kirkby Fleetham Hall, Kirkby Fleetham, The North 38
Lake Vyrnwy, Llanwddyn, Wales 54
Little Thakeham, Storrington, Sussex 180
Llwynderw, Abergwesyn, Wales 56
Lords of the Manor, Upper Slaughter, The Cotswolds 84
Lower Brook House, Blockley, The Cotswolds 86
The Lygon Arms, Broadway, The Cotswolds 88
Lythe Hill Hotel, Haslemere, London & Home Counties 114
Maison Talbooth, Dedham, East Anglia 128
Mallory Court, Bishop's Tachbrook, Central England 66
The Manor House, Castle Combe, The South-West 166
Michael's Nook, Grasmere, The North 40
Miller Howe, Windermere, The North 42
Number Sixteen Hotel, London, London & Home Counties 116
The Orient Express, London-Venice, London & Home Counties 118
Prior's Hall, Stebbing, East Anglia 130
The Priory Country House, Rushlake Green, Sussex 182
Riber Hall, Matlock, Central England 68
The Ritz, London, London & Home Counties 120
The Riverside, Helford, Cornwall 150
The Riverside Country House, Ashford-in-the-Water, Central England 70
The Royal Crescent Hotel, Bath, Avon 98
Seckford Hall Hotel, Woodbridge, East Anglia 132
The Sharrow Bay Country House, Ullswater, The North 44
Shipdham Place, Shipdham, East Anglia 134
The Sign of the Angel, Lacock, The South-West 168
The Stafford Hotel, London, London & Home Counties 122
Ston Easton Park, Farrington Gurney, Avon 100
Stone Green Hall, Mersham, Kent 184
Sunlaws House Hotel, Kelso, Scotland 32
The Swan, Bibury, The Cotswolds 90
Swynford Paddocks, Newmarket, East Anglia 136
Tarr Steps Hotel, Hawkridge, The South-West 170
Thornbury Castle, Thornbury, Avon 102
White Moss House, Rydal Water, The North 46
Woodhayes, Whimple, Devon 152

Index by Town

Abergwesyn, Wales 56
Ashford, Kent 176
Ashford-in-the-Water, Central England 70
Aston Clinton, London & Home Counties 106
Bath, Avon 98
Beaminster, The South-West 162
Beanacre, The South-West 156
Bibury, The Cotswolds 90
Bishop's Tachbrook, Central England 66
Blockley, The Cotswolds 86
Broadway, The Cotswolds 78, 88
Buckland, The Cotswolds 74
Castle Combe, The South-West 166
Chagford, Devon 142, 146
Climping, Sussex 174
Coatham Mundeville, The North 36
Dedham, East Anglia 128
Dunblane, Scotland 22
East Grinstead, Sussex 178
Farrington Gurney, Avon 100
Fort William, Scotland 26
Gittisham, Devon 144
Grasmere, *see also* Rydal Water, The North 40
Grimston, *see* Kings Lynn
Gullane, Scotland 24
Haslemere, London & Home Counties 114
Hawkridge, The South-West 170
Helford, Cornwall 150
Hinton Charterhouse, Avon 94
Humbie, Scotland 30
Hunstrete, Avon 96
Kelso, Scotland 32
Kilchrenan, Scotland 18
Kings Lynn, East Anglia 126
Kirkby Fleetham, The North 38
Lacock, The South-West 168
Ledaig, Scotland 28
Ledbury, Central England 64
Llandudno, Wales 50
Llanwddyn, Wales 54

London, London & Home Counties   108, 110, 116-122
Malvern Wells, Central England   60
Matlock, Central England   68
Mersham, Kent   184
Nairn, Scotland   20
New Milton, The South-West   164
Newmarket, East Anglia   136
Northallerton, *see* Kirkby Fleetham
Oakham, Central England   62
Penzance, Cornwall   140
Rushlake Green, Sussex   182
Rydal Water, The North   46
Sheepwash, Devon   148
Shipdham, East Anglia   134
Shurdington, The Cotswolds   82
Sonning-on-Thames, London & Home Counties   112
Stebbing, East Anglia   130
Storrington, Sussex   180
Taunton, The South-West   160
Tetbury, The Cotswolds   76, 80
Thornbury, Avon   102
Ullswater, The North   44
Upper Slaughter, The Cotswolds   84
Warminster, The South-West   158
Whimple, Devon   152
Whitebrook, Wales   52
Windermere, The North   42
Woodbridge, East Anglia   132

Authors' Biographies

Richard Nissen was born in 1949 and educated at Shrewsbury School, the Sorbonne and University College London where he studied architecture. The idea for the book came when he was looking for a hotel for his honeymoon...

Roger Lacoste-England is a director of a London-based planning and development company, but for many years he worked with the WHO and the World Bank planning and implementing medical care services. He has visited over 30 countries and travels widely (trying to avoid modern hotels and international food!). He now lives in London and Provence.

Alison Hoblyn trained as an interior designer at Brighton College of Art and Design, but is also interested in graphics. This is the first book she has illustrated.

Marina Tobias is writing a book about food. She lives in London and travels as often as possible, preferably with a romantic companion.